The Orgasm Fantasy

THE ORGASM FANTASY

Improving Sex and Relationships

Dr. Ofer Grosbard

IPBOOKS.net
International Psychoanalytic Books

International Psychoanalytic Books (IPBooks)
New York • http://www.IPBooks.net

The Orgasm Fantasy

Published by International Psychoanalytic Books (IPBooks)
Queens, NY
Online at www.IPBooks.net

Book cover design by
Book design and formatting services by Noel S. Morado

ISBN: 978-1-949093-88-9

I'd like to live in a world in which, when people shake hands to introduce themselves, they also tell each other their orgasm fantasies. Then we would more easily get to know, understand, and accept one another.

(The author)

orgasmfantasy.com

The Orgasm Fantasy – A New Social Movement

TABLE OF CONTENTS

Personality Theory of the Orgasm Fantasy

Conscious Thinking
Orgasm Fantasy
Dreams

PREFACE

Orgasm Fantasy Theory is an applied theory of personality that invites a person to become familiar with the three main levels of thinking that comprise his personality – nighttime dreams, the orgasm fantasy, and conscious thought – in order to better know himself and how he encounters and interacts with the world. The case studies presented in the book to illustrate the theory were drawn from different sources: the author's clinic, case presentations and discussions with colleagues, and the psychoanalytic literature.[1] The clinical material that appears in the book is authentic; only the patient's identifying details have been changed. Thus any resemblance between a patient described here and an actual person is purely coincidental. In the section on "Improving sex and relationships" after every case study, the author has added descriptions from his own imagination to illustrate how the lessons from each case study may be applied. The case studies are arranged from the milder to the more serious. Separate chapters are devoted to

---

[1] See the bibliography at the end of the book.

homosexuality and guidance for parents. Awareness of our three levels of thinking can help us not only in our relationship with our partner or other adults, but also in raising better-adjusted children. In the afterword, the reader will find a brief discussion of six issues of special importance.

The Unconscious First Level of Thinking – Dreams

Every night each of us becomes a great artist: We create full-length movies of which we are the director, screenwriter, casting director, and also the set designer. Then in the morning we awaken and erase all our hard work. Does this make any sense? We need to recognize that while we sleep we live an emotional life that is just as intensive as the emotional life of our waking hours, and we shouldn't ignore this other life. We should try to remember our dreams, write them down, and attempt to understand them. This is not a complicated process and requires only minimal practice. The mere act of listening to our dreams makes us more creative people. Suddenly we will begin to understand the nuances of our feelings that are repressed during the day and slip into our dreams at night. Suddenly, too, we will grasp how associations work. These are the heart and soul of a dream in which one thing calls to mind another, and we allow ourselves to play more freely with our imaginations. All this comes from listening to our dreams. How often have new ideas and thoughts come to us in dreams or just while lying in bed in the dark when thinking is freer and more associative? At these times a person is not occupied with putting his thoughts in logical order but rather is closer to his feelings, and suddenly things become clearer.

I personally had the good fortune to undergo therapy with a therapist who encouraged the exploration of dreams. For over two years, I kept a detailed dream journal and brought my dreams to each session. I discovered that I had a world inside me whose existence I'd been unaware of. I would never have come to really know and understand myself without the revelation of this hidden world. No amount of talking over many years of therapy in any verbal language about my feelings could have competed with this rich dream world that depicts my emotions in a precise symbolic language of images, my own personal language. Also, there are many things we can't talk about simply because we are unaware of their existence. But our dreams are well aware of them. In my work with patients, I look for characteristic elements of dreams - for emotions that recur within this rich dream world. One person may have paranoid dreams, another dreams filled with anxiety, and another consumed with guilt in his dreams. A patient's profound emotional dependence on others may only become apparent through his or her dreams. Yet another may find that he is always laughing in his dreams. These central themes are revealed after we have written down our dreams for some time (though not for too long) and are crucially important in helping us understand our inclinations. Sometimes these central themes are not entirely clear and the process can take somewhat longer. Often there will be several different themes, some of which may be contradictory (e.g., dreams about success along with dreams about failure).

Just as each of us has a unique overt personality, we also have certain trends in our dream world that we need to identify. Patience is important here. But we now have our Archimedes' Point, that point of reference outside ourselves that enables us to observe ourselves and to bring about change. We are now more conscious of our tendencies and more ready to take responsibility for them. My impression is that many therapists don't work enough on their own dreams. Many have never kept a dream journal over an extended period, making it difficult for them to give this gift to their patients. Contemporary psychological theories also place less emphasis on dreams. I can, however, attest that in many instances the breakthrough in understanding a patient occurred through uncovering his or her dream world.

Until now we have not been talking about the interpretation of dreams, but rather how to relate to the overt content of the main dream themes that characterize our personalities. We now turn to discuss the hidden emotional content of dreams.

How do we work on a dream? First, a dream is a product of the residue of the previous day, such as something that happened to us or a thought that was repressed for various reasons. The emotion that we experienced was unpleasant, we were preoccupied with other things, although pleasant it was something we felt was impossible, something we criticized ourselves for, etc. Dreams may be either pleasant or unpleasant. Sometimes we have suppressed a wish, and sometimes anxiety. This emotional content is largely expressed in a symbolic language of images, a private language we have developed in the course of our lives.

Thus the traditional question about a dream, "what does this make you think of?" is an appropriate and correct one. It is also true that only the patient can really know the source of his or her dream. An experienced therapist who knows his or her patients well can certainly conduct a dialogue with them on this subject and make suggestions that will often be helpful in advancing their understanding. The final arbiter, of course, is the patient. He or she must have the feeling that "the penny has dropped." This often occurs as a flash of insight in which all the pieces of the puzzle have fallen into place and the dream and its origins have been understood.

It is often worth paying attention to what the patient related to just prior to or following recounting the dream. Why did he suddenly recall the dream? Or, perhaps, what did the dream remind him of? The solution may sometimes be found there. In focusing on this associative thinking, the therapist listens to what issues lead to recalling other issues, rather than focusing on the dream story as a whole and its overt content.

A dream, however, is far more than this. The main themes of our dreams are also the internal prison in which we are locked, a constant translation of external events into our unique personal code, a recurrent experiential world that characterizes us, a bit like a fish that thinks there is nothing but water around it. In the book, therefore, we will meet John, who translates many situations in his life into loneliness; Luna, who no matter what happens in her life, feels that she is in control of things and is also rescuing her mother; Samuel, for whom each external event is a trigger for his next creative invention; and Lisa who feels repeated humiliation, even when she has attained love. In order to uncover these hidden themes of an internal experience it is not even necessary to identify the origins of the dream in the preceding day; rather, it is sufficient to examine the overt content of the dream.

For the most part, dreams change slowly and incrementally over many years. Sometimes we are lucky, and witness in the course of therapy the process of dreams changing relatively rapidly. When this change endures and echoes a change in reality, it can indicate deep and meaningful change for the patient. Samuel dreamed about a scary puppet that resembled his mother. Gradually, he began to fear her less until he was not afraid to confront her in his dream. The change in his real life was not long in coming.

I like patients to lie on the couch. As Freud said, this situation naturally stimulates more associative thinking. This way, as we embark on a journey together, neither of us is distracted by facial expressions that can be inhibiting or misleading. Sometimes I close my eyes so as to be better attuned to my own associations that could possibly serve the patient.

Delving into dreams makes a person more creative, and it has a similar effect on therapy. The underlying message is that there is more inside me than I imagine, and that it is okay for me to feel and freely express my thoughts and associations. "Tell me everything that goes through your mind, even if it's clever, silly or embarrassing." This is the basic directive of psychoanalysis that I have found to be particularly effective.

I feel I remember patients more by their dreams than by events in their lives. Sometimes the patient brings a formative dream that explains a deep conflict in his personality, the kind of dream that stays with us for a long time. The same happens with recurrent dreams. I advise my patients to keep a notebook or cell phone next to their bed and to start writing down or recording their dreams as soon as they wake up, before they lose the thread. Sometimes I ask them if they had a dream that week that they remember. In this way I teach them to pay attention to themselves, to listen to themselves and to respect what they have created. Indeed, one of the main goals of therapy is for patients to be able to play more, to create more, and to fulfill themselves and their inherent potential. To this end, obstacles need to be removed, and dreams do this very well.

The Second Level of Thinking – The Orgasm Fantasy

The orgasm fantasy is the most stimulating fantasy a person has, one that brings him or her to a sexual climax. Usually it is experienced during masturbation when a person is alone and free to imagine anything. But it can certainly also be brought to mind during intercourse or at any other time. In the psychoanalytic literature it is known as the Central Masturbation Fantasy[2]

---

[2] Laufer, M. (1976). The Central Masturbation Fantasy, the Final Sexual Organization, and Adolescence. Psychoanal. St. Child, 31, 297–316.

and depicts what is regarded as a person's Final Sexual Organization. I have chosen this name, the Orgasm Fantasy, to highlight the unique and powerful physiological change that this imagery may bring about. It is hard to imagine another fantasy whose objective is such a dramatic physiological change.

The first natural law of human behavior arising from the "imprinting" of the orgasm fantasy is that the emotional core of the relations depicted in the orgasm fantasy does not change over the course of a person's life.

What is interesting is that while the content of the fantasy, the "action," may change, the emotional hallmarks of the relations between the actors within it remain constant.[3] For example, if a man achieves satisfaction when he whips a woman and dominates her, he may also achieve satisfaction when he takes her from behind and dominates her. The story that is told in the orgasm fantasy may vary, but not the type of relationship that underlies it.

The second natural law of human behavior arising from the "imprinting" of the orgasm fantasy is that we tend to reenact and relive the type of emotional relationship that is revealed in our orgasm fantasy in our daily lives, with people of both sexes.

This is our default reaction, an automatic personal and rapid response when we don't have time for the more complex third level of conscious thinking. We tend to use

---

[3] The literature review at the end of the book confirms this, and is also backed by the author's personal experience with many patients. Even though the writers do not indicate this explicitly, it is evident from their detailed case studies.

this response in relations with close family members as well as in moments of stress, which is why it is so vitally important that we familiarize ourselves with and come to understand our orgasm fantasy. For example, the man described above who in his orgasm fantasy is whipping a woman, will tend to quickly react with anger in many different situations.

Presumably the emotional core of this fantasy starts to develop at a very young age, possibly in the second year of life, as a result of the parental bond, and is imprinted in us as our default relationship with those around us for the rest of our lives. The significance of imprinting is that a critical period exists for consolidating a particular behavior that then remains fixed in a person's life. From the time of its creation, the orgasm fantasy shapes our behavior, usually outside our awareness. In adolescence, however, it may become apparent during masturbation or sexual relations. It will often take many more years for the person to become fully conscious of the orgasm fantasy, if he or she ever does, the reason being that the content of the fantasy, while sexually pleasurable, may be destructive to one's self-image and is therefore suppressed within the unconscious. Some thus claim they do not have any sexual fantasies, or that they cannot point to a fantasy that arouses them the most.

The unique power of a single fantasy is clear, in that the type of relations it depicts is something that constantly accompanies us throughout our lives and is responsible for some significant areas of our behavior. Dreams, as noted above, can change slowly and to a small extent during the course of our lives, as may various conscious tendencies of our thinking (depression, anxiety, anger, etc.). In dreams, as in conscious thinking, we may identify several central currents that characterize us. However, when a single fantasy maintains a constant presence throughout life, the kind of emotional relationship that emerges in this fantasy will have an enormous impact on our relationships with the people around us. The orgasm fantasy is thus above all a relationship fantasy whose importance far exceeds its sexual context.

One example of the consolidation of the orgasm fantasy in early childhood, prior to reaching the awareness that takes place in adolescence, is that of people (both men and women) with homosexual tendencies. Such people may have orgasm fantasies in which relationships include various emotional characteristics that occur with members of the same sex. We know that these homosexual tendencies are crystallized very early in life (there may also be a genetic component involved here) and do not change in the course of a person's life. Signs of these tendencies may be evident in boys and girls of preschool and elementary school age. During this period, when boys tend to associate with other boys and girls with other girls, those with homosexual tendencies will tend to form friendships with members of the opposite sex. In adolescence, the opposite will occur for both groups. Thus, not only do relationships within the orgasm fantasy become fixed at a very young age, but so does the gender of the object of this fantasy.

People can be attracted to members of their own sex (homosexuals), members of the opposite sex (heterosexuals) or to both (bisexuals) in an endless variety of fantasies. Bear in mind that what interests us here is the type of relationship that is created in the fantasy and not the content of the story itself or the particular person to whom the individual is attracted. Bisexuals will also tend to build the same type of relationship whether they are picturing women or men in their orgasm fantasy, and will reenact this type of relationship with other people in their lives.

How does the orgasm fantasy take shape in the interaction between child and parent? For an outside observer it is not easy to get into a baby's mind and imagine what he is imagining. We do, however, have one lead to go on – the orgasm fantasy. One young woman reports that she achieves a climax when she imagines that she is being beaten. This fantasy does not necessarily mean that she was ever beaten. But it's quite possible that the emotional dynamic that became fixed in her orgasm fantasy is one in which someone is angry at her or scolding her. How did this come about? Her mother or father may have often looked at her in an accusing, or perhaps only a critical manner. At such moments, this child senses a certain kind of connection to the parent. Another possibility is that she was ignored much of the time and her way of attracting attention was to do forbidden things for which she would be rebuked. Later in life, this girl will tend, largely unconsciously, to imagine that others are angry with her, or to provoke anger in others so as to reenact and relive this feeling. Again we see that it is not the story itself that the person invented that matters, but rather the nature of the feelings that characterize the relationship between the characters.

Or take a young man who imagines that the woman in his orgasm fantasy trusts him completely. He pictures himself undressing her, sees the look of trust in her eyes and then achieves climax. He is surely reenacting a key emotion that developed between him and his caregiver parent at a critical stage in the formation of the orgasm fantasy. This person will tend to trust other people and therefore could often be hurt when this trust is not reciprocated.

Often, however, identifying the emotion hidden in the orgasm fantasy requires deeper exploration. Take, for example, a man who achieves climax when he sees a woman's hands beckoning to him. Only when asked why this woman is calling him does he tell us that, in his mind, she is calling him because he is a good boy. How did he come to have this particular orgasm fantasy? His mother had postpartum depression and gave him little attention. He tried to be a good boy so that she would call him to come and be near her. Throughout his life he will keep trying to be a good boy and to please the people around him.

Another girl will achieve climax when she imagines in her orgasm fantasy that she is secretly spying on her masturbating boyfriend. An in-depth examination of this story reveals that for her he is the important central figure and that she feels small next to him, observing him. This is not relations between equals. She achieves satisfaction through him, by identifying with his satisfaction, and is thus dependent on him. She even seems embarrassed by this dependence and therefore keeps herself hidden. We may surmise that in early childhood this girl tried to observe the parent caring for her and adapt herself to him or her. She was the little one and he or she the important one, the leader, and her pleasure came through the parent. This girl did not have a parent who sees her, places her at the center and adapts himself or herself to her. In her life she will have difficulty assuming a central role and will let others lead her, at least in her automatic default behavior. Another girl, however, could have the same fantasy of watching her boyfriend masturbate, but with a very different meaning. Hence, finding out what emotion underlies the fantasy is of utmost importance.

The variety and richness of orgasm fantasies is endless. Just as no thought or dream is impossible, no orgasm fantasy is impossible. People can imagine stories that have no sexual content whatsoever and find themselves aroused, while others may be aroused by things we would consider as unimaginably perverse. Still others may picture romantic love stories. There are no good or bad fantasies. Throughout this book, we will see that the type of relationship manifested in a person's orgasm fantasy can serve that person positively or negatively, depending on the circumstances. In any event, sometime in our earliest years, this fantasy was the solution we developed and it proved to be effective in our relationship with our parent caregiver.

The following are several examples of orgasm fantasies illustrating the idea that the key element of the fantasy is the quality of the relationship that is developed between the characters and not the sexual story itself. Evidently, in our early life a powerful primal relationship pattern developed between us and the parent caregiver, and our developing sexuality simply "hitched a ride" on it. In other words, our sexuality exploited the power of this primal relationship in order to come into being. These relationships, therefore, have relevance for the individual far beyond the sexual context. Consider, for example, a teenage boy who climaxes when he pictures himself as a goalkeeper who keeps failing to save the incoming shots, a decidedly humiliating experience. This boy had masochistic personality traits and tended to irritate his friends, causing them to lash out at him and hurt him. Only later did this boy come to associate the balls penetrating the net in his orgasm fantasy with himself being penetrated. Another person achieved sexual satisfaction by imagining he had a factory in which he completely controlled all the precision machinery. At the peak of exerting this control he climaxed. In his daily life, he constantly tried to control the people in his world. Another girl would achieve satisfaction when she imagined boys wanting to sleep with her and turning them down. This girl showed clear sadistic tendencies in her daily life. The orgasm fantasy is thus, in essence, a relationship fantasy.

Often the patients' orgasm fantasy accompanies them into the therapist's office. We will meet Jacob, who comes into the room looking at the floor, afraid to make direct eye contact. In his orgasm fantasy, a woman dominates him. Avery,[4] on the other hand, enters the clinic holding herself erect, exuding a strong presence. She will later relate that during sex it's important for her to be on top, and that in her relationship with her husband she is the one "who wears the pants in the family." Maya comes in, pauses in the center of the room and

---

[4] Participated in parental-guidance sessions and is not included in the case studies appearing in the book.

smiles before sitting down, inviting the therapist to take a good look at her. In her orgasm fantasy she is being watched as she showers. In life she has a strong desire for people to notice her. Another man strolls into the clinic brimming with self-confidence, as if he were walking into his own home. In his orgasm fantasy he pictures a relationship with young, even very young, girls, over whom he has total control. In his work as well, it's important for him to be the boss, the one who controls everything.

Such is the orgasm fantasy, our primal encounter with the world. Unlike dreams, this second layer of thinking embodies a primal response to reality. The first year in a child's life is largely nonverbal and in this way it resembles dreams. The orgasm fantasy is also primarily a story in pictures, but sometimes has a more developed verbal component (people may imagine hearing certain words that arouse them) as well as, most crucially, a recurring pattern of a real relationship. Hence, the hypothesis (still in need of corroboration) is that it develops in the second year of a child's life.

In other respects, the orgasm fantasy may be compared to dreams which, as we know, have both overt action and covert emotional meaning. The same is true of the orgasm fantasy, in which there is an overt story, but the part that really interests us is the hidden part, the emotional ties between the characters in the fantasy.

Where does the content of our orgasm fantasy originate? The fantasy draws on a stockpile of events with a sexual connotation that we encountered in the course of our lives in order to bring the emotional message to life. The process works in a similar way to dreams that use our private stockpile of imagery in order to convey an emotional message.

To the best of my knowledge, therapists generally give little thought to the orgasm fantasy, and certainly do not ascribe to it the meaning and significance that I note here. This I believe is a pity. The great advantage of the orgasm fantasy, as with dreams, lies in a person's ability to take responsibility for these aspects of himself. The person comes to understand that if throughout his life he imagines the same kind of thing with the same type of relationships, all of his own accord without anyone asking him to do so, this surely has significance. Unlike dreams, the orgasm fantasy is conscious and overt and the relationships in it repeat themselves exactly, and therein lies its power.

Needless to say, being conscious of the orgasm fantasy and accepting its legitimacy in the world of the imagination and play, can not only substantially improve a couple's sex life, but also improve their relationship by making them more aware of their own and their partner's personal inclinations.

On first hearing about their partner's orgasm fantasy, people often feel that many things suddenly make sense. Something that for years they couldn't quite manage to put into words now emerges as a single, focused story. I can also confirm that being exposed to a patient's orgasm fantasy in the clinic can often serve as a breakthrough in understanding him or her. Getting to know people's orgasm fantasy can help us understand and accept them, because then we will also realize what underlies their behavior and not ascribe hidden meanings or negative personal motivations to it.

Should we not all come out of the closet and reveal our orgasm fantasy, even if it may not be exactly flattering? If gay men, lesbians or other LGBTQ people refuse to acknowledge their sexuality, including that within their orgasm fantasy, their lives are likely to be phony and empty. The same is true for all of us if we conceal from ourselves our orgasm fantasy which offers critical information for understanding our unique encounter with the world. As there are endless possibilities of the orgasm fantasy, and apparently no two people share the exact orgasm fantasy, personal discovery and tolerance for the other become all the more vital.

How do we discover our orgasm fantasy? This can be harder for people who tend to repress their emotions. Masturbation is one way. During masturbation we should try to freely and fearlessly imagine all sorts of scenes and see which arouses us the most. Sometimes pornographic movies with diverse contents can give us a direction. But ultimately no porno movie will compare with the movie that we ourselves create and which accurately depicts our orgasm fantasy. Many people have a general idea. They only need to fine-tune it, to be precise about it and find the most arousing story. Then the tremendous power of this orgasm-inducing story will help them take ownership of it, at which point they will realize that they have found the key to one of the most important hidden chambers of their being.

A few words for the many people who find it hard to discover their orgasm fantasy. Even people who are familiar with their orgasm fantasy may find it difficult to activate this imagery. Our defenses can impede our ability to fantasize. Thus, in the midst of the orgasm fantasy, thoughts may intrude, such as "This isn't real" or "It's just a fantasy" or even "Am I out of my mind?!" The objective of these defensive thoughts is to prevent us from losing touch with reality. And indeed, many people find it hard to set aside, even momentarily, the constraints of their daily reality. Such people will have trouble discovering their orgasm fantasy. What can be done in such cases?

Each person needs to find his or her own way. Some will be able to discover their orgasm fantasy when they are on vacation, far from their everyday tasks and with the opportunity to focus on themselves. They may then find time to masturbate, watch porno films, or play sexual games with their partner. Others may actually be more open to this discovery when they are very tired, because that's when their defenses are lowered, while for yet others, the early morning when they are feeling refreshed and ready to tackle new assignments may be the most opportune time.

One woman discovered her orgasm fantasy when her husband announced that he wanted a divorce, which freed her to say, "What do I care?" She masturbated and found herself imagining a highly arousing fantasy she'd never allowed herself to entertain. This was a very high-functioning woman, firmly anchored in reality, and always concerned about what others would say. It's no wonder that it was difficult for her to let go and discover her orgasm fantasy when she was so attuned to the opinions of others.

Another man was unable to use his aggressive orgasm fantasy, of which he was aware, when his wife was being nice to him. He asked her to deliberately do something to anger him, and was then able to get uninhibited pleasure from his orgasm fantasy.

Sometimes wine or marijuana can help. I don't, however, recommend relying on drugs; better to develop the imagination. Similarly, I would advise someone who is having physical problems with sexual intercourse (difficulty getting or maintaining an erection, vaginal discomfort, etc.) to work on developing their imagination rather than resorting to chemical remedies.

Most of us are functioning individuals firmly rooted in everyday reality, and may have difficulty immersing ourselves in a fantasy world. People with a hysterical personality will certainly find it easier to discover their orgasm fantasy than those with an obsessive personality. The former allow themselves to be more associative and colorful in their thinking, rather than clinging strongly to the minutiae of everyday life. Many of us have lost contact with ourselves, preferring to dwell on how we function in the world and how we have dealt with reality over the years. Many people stopped listening to themselves long ago, to the point that their orgasm fantasy has ceased to interest them, and they consciously choose a dull daily life devoid of fantasies. The more stable, protected and organized individuals are in their daily lives, the less chance of them being carried away by their fantasies. People who are struggling with things are often the ones who are more alert to their orgasm fantasy and more able to enjoy it.

When and how should one ask a patient to divulge their orgasm fantasy? This is a question that is practically guaranteed to be awkward for both therapist and patient.

Even long-term therapy often concludes without any discussion of the patient's orgasm fantasy. Because the patient's orgasm fantasy is a powerful tool for advancing therapy, it is advantageous to learn about it as soon as possible. Still, it's hard to say precisely when this question should be raised. It depends on the therapist, the patient, and the relationship that develops between them.

Each therapist and patient has to find the right time. Often, but not necessarily, it will be easier when the therapist and patient have known each other for some time. When the patient is a young male and the therapist an older woman, or when the patient is a young woman and the therapist an older man, the patient may wait for the therapist to raise the issue as confirmation to proceed. Without help and guidance from the therapist, patients may find it difficult to raise this subject voluntarily. A therapist who asks this question at an early stage of therapy, possibly even as part of the intake interview together with other questions, some of which may also be embarrassing, conveys a message that this is an important subject that can be talked about. The therapist who in the intake interview asks about the patient's thoughts – nighttime dreams, conscious thoughts and orgasm fantasies – is sending the important message that the orgasm fantasy should not be set apart from all other thoughts just because it may be more embarrassing. During the conversation, the therapist may of course explain to the patient that the importance of the orgasm fantasy goes well beyond the sexual context and that it reflects an important aspect of someone's interpersonal relations in general. Above all, the message to patients is that it is up to them to determine the pace, and that they may choose not to answer this question at present, or in the future. In my experience, most patients understand and appreciate this, and are pleased to cooperate.

The Conscious Third Level of Thinking

People have different tendencies of thinking in their waking lives. Some remain angry all or most of the time, thinking about a remark someone made to them and how they're going to get revenge. They might imagine themselves cursing or hitting the other person. Others may be consumed by anxiety, and others may feel guilty or unworthy most of the time for years on end. As with dreams, a person can generally identify more than one major theme, and just as no dream is impossible, no conscious thought is impossible.

In other words, even though each of us may have many different dreams or conscious thoughts, it is the major themes that shape our personality and our response to the world. Indeed, similar to dreams, since everyone has a unique personality, so he or she has one or more central themes in the conscious third level of thinking. While it is often difficult to decide which of these unconscious and conscious thought currents are more dominant, it doesn't really matter; it is sufficient to be aware of their existence. These thought currents during dreams and wakefulness tend to change slowly and incrementally over time. Thus we find much similarity between the first, unconscious, level of thinking and the third, conscious, level of thinking – except for the well-accepted difference that the first level is called a primal process and is based on associative thinking, while the third level is based on secondary thinking that is essentially organized and logical.

Some people have daydreams that recur regularly over many years. A daydream is a story we tell ourselves while awake; we are aware we are fantasizing and that it is not real. In a dream, however, we feel that what is happening is real. A frequently recurring daydream is just one possible current of our conscious thinking and it may be pleasant or unpleasant. One example of a classic daydream is that of an athlete who, ahead of a competition, envisions himself standing on the podium, being awarded a medal in front of the cheering crowd. Another person will keep fantasizing that she is a movie star or famous singer on stage and picture in her mind exactly what she does there. Yet another may regularly imagine that he keeps failing his exams even though he actually does well in them. Throughout the book, we will encounter the daydreams of different patients and come to see the connection between these daydreams and the unconscious first level of dreams and the second level of the orgasm fantasy.

As we will see, there is a constant flow of content between the different levels of thinking. Thoughts from the conscious third level are repressed into the unconscious first level and surface into a person's awareness at different moments and in different contexts. Often the conscious third level of thinking compensates for or complements the second level, the orgasm fantasy.

The orgasm fantasy itself may be consolidated in early childhood from a response to currents in the unconscious first level of thinking or, as we have seen, may be repressed there when it harms a person's self-image. Put simply, there is a continual flow of content between the various levels of thinking, and reciprocal relations of opposition or balance between them. In the descriptions of the different cases, the reader will encounter this interplay among the three thinking levels.

How does the conscious third level of thinking develop? This is the highest level, which enables us to undertake more complex thinking. Responses from this level to the surrounding reality will thus be slower and more processed. Often these are responses to various social situations, thoughts that contain logical aspects or are based on previous knowledge. Third-level conscious thinking is different from the impulse-driven and personally-directed default of the orgasm fantasy although it is not always easy to differentiate between them.

Familiarity with the orgasm fantasy as well as with a person's conscious streams of thought will help us in making this distinction. This conscious third level of thinking is, of course, shaped by the relationship with one's parents following (or perhaps also parallel to) the shaping of the orgasm fantasy. This level contains new aspects of identification with the parents on various issues as well as responses to the two lower levels of thinking. As we shall see, the conscious third level of thinking is responsible for many of our behaviors and decisions in life.

The two higher levels of thinking, the orgasm fantasy and conscious thought, shape our encounter with reality, which is not the case with the unconscious first level of thinking. The orgasm fantasy, however, will always be personal, while the conscious level of thinking will also include other elements such as values and conforming to social norms.

Without exploration by the therapist of the conscious third level of thinking, this material may remain inaccessible to therapist and patient, because the patient is accustomed to his ways of thinking and is often completely unaware of the extent to which it characterizes him. For example, he may think that everyone goes around feeling angry all the time, or not be aware that this is actually what he often does. Another possibility is that the patient is ashamed of this material.

Orgasm Fantasy Theory thus invites us to turn our attention to our three levels of thinking, of which we are sometimes unaware, so that we may realize our inherent potential. The examples in the book will illuminate how this can operate.

A dream of mine about this book: I organized a masquerade ball in a house whose address contained the number 46. During the ball I lifted everyone's masks and their true faces were revealed. I was there without a mask. When I woke up I understood that my orgasm fantasy theory removes people's masks, and that I have already removed mine. I still wasn't sure where the number 46 came from. A few weeks later, when I was going over the material for this book, I came to Samuel's dream. In his dream he is hiking in a canyon. His father is walking ahead of him wearing a shirt with the number 23 on it. Samuel searches for an adult at the head of the line to join up with and finds someone wearing the number 46. The man's graying hair makes him think that it's me. In therapy, he came to understand that he is searching for a father substitute and wants to identify with me.

This young man, as you will see, is extremely creative. He assigned me the number 46 and now my creation takes place in a house with this number. Samuel impresses me, and I greatly enjoy our talks and his interesting dreams. Is he making me, his therapist, creative? That is how I feel in the dream. Of course, I let him read what I wrote about him; he was quite moved and thanked me profusely.

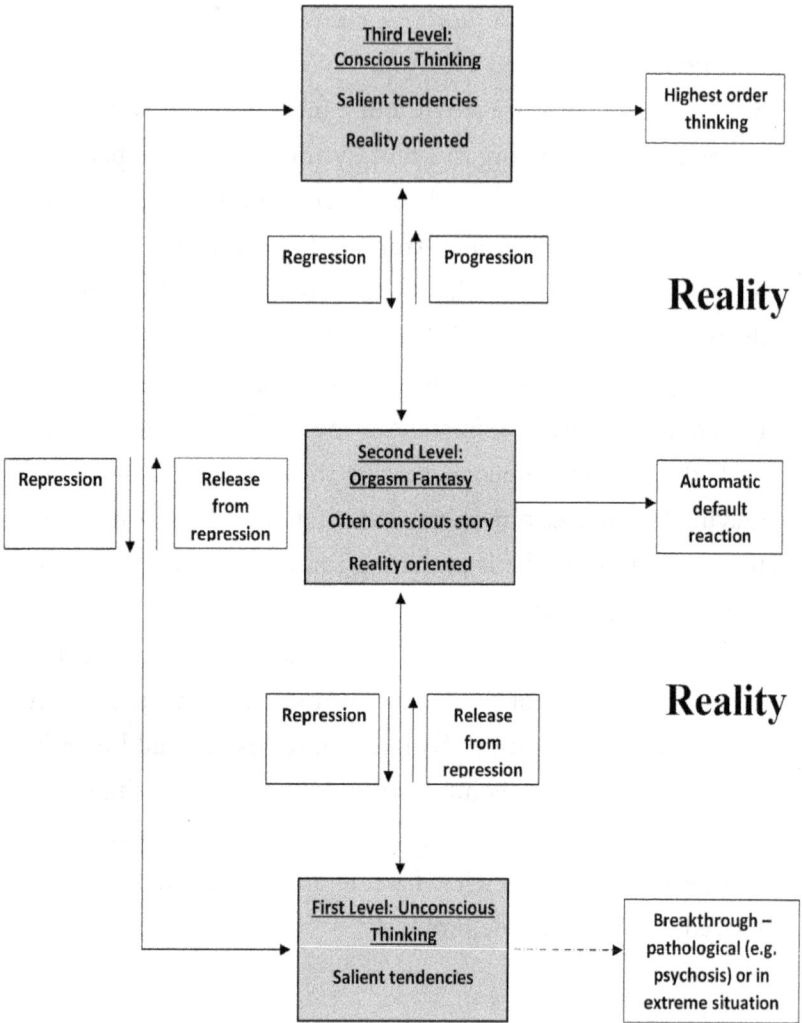

Personality Structure According to Orgasm Fantasy Theory: Three Levels of Thinking

CASE STUDIES

1. SPANKING

Emily was unable to achieve sexual satisfaction until her forties. Only then did she suddenly discover her orgasm fantasy. In this fantasy, a man was spanking her. The fantasy had several variations. In one, he was spanking her while scolding her for what she had done. It's wasn't the pain that was significant, she thinks, but rather the feeling of being chastised. Sometimes the spanker was her father, sometimes a teacher she admired, and sometimes the woman in the fantasy was not her but someone she didn't know. There were also several variations in the scene she imagined and in the plot development, but what all this new imagery had in common was that her orgasm occurred at the moment of peak humiliation.

Emily came to see that this fantasy that was sexually pleasurable but destructive to her self-image had been repressed for many years. She now felt she had the secret key to her orgasm treasure chest – a very specific fantasy that had been hiding somewhere in her unconscious until it finally surfaced when she was apparently ready to recognize and accept it.

Emily warmly embraced this discovery, began masturbating frequently, trying out different imaginary scenarios, testing and exploring the limits of her fantasy. She noticed that the details of the fantasy could change but not the humiliating relationship that was the sole trigger for her orgasm. She also noticed that this experience of humiliation had remained constant over the years.

This exciting discovery was accompanied by another equally exciting discovery. Emily observed that her relationships with men often followed this same masochistic pattern, and realized that this was possibly the reason she had trouble forming a strong and stable relationship. For example, when her partner warmly caressed and praised her she might react unpleasantly, even aggressively. But when he admonished her, she often thought she was getting the punishment she deserved. At times, she sensed that she was deliberately angering him in order for him to respond in kind, while at other times, she would apologize unnecessarily as if she had done something terrible. These were subtleties, her deeply private secrets that she had never previously contemplated, and that now suddenly made sense in the context of her orgasm fantasy that had revealed itself in all its glory. Emily understood that she was reenacting her orgasm fantasy with her romantic partners and realized that this could be the reason for her never being able to establish a stable, long-term relationship.

One revelation followed another. Emily saw that she was also reenacting the mechanism of the orgasm fantasy at work with her colleagues and bosses, both male and female. This situation occurred whenever she reacted automatically to something, her default response. She would thus blame herself for things that went wrong that were outside her area of responsibility, and when her work was appreciated, her automatic response would be to feel that the praise was undeserved. If I would just stop and think about it, she told herself later, I might not react this way.

Emily's friends had long been telling her that her sexual behavior was harming her but she didn't really understand what they meant. She would push the men she met into bed before they'd even considered it. She told her girlfriends that she just wanted to see if they clicked in the bedroom since sex is such an important criterion for a relationship's success, so why wait. When she first met someone she actually liked, she blurted out in the middle of their conversation: "Come on, let's fuck." The guy was shocked. They did sleep together but never went out again. Only now does Emily seem to understand what lies behind her behavior.

Improving sex and relationships

Emily gradually realized that she had no reason to be ashamed of her orgasm fantasy or of who she is. On the contrary, it was better for her to acknowledge this fantasy and put its tremendous power to good use. She began to share her orgasm fantasy with her partners, encouraging them to tell her theirs and suggesting that they play out these fantasies in the bedroom with the sky being the limit. Emily, who until recently had never experienced orgasm, reached sexual heights that she vividly described as "explosions of divine revelation." The great sex made her and her partners feel closer. By overcoming any embarrassment and sharing their orgasm fantasies, they were able to more fully accept one another.

Moreover, having become cognizant of the masochistic element of her orgasm fantasy and the destructive way she handled her relationships, Emily is now able to control how the fantasy affects her daily interactions rather than letting it control her. She also shared this difficulty with her partners and asked them to be mindful of her weakness. These conversations helped Emily and her different partners – and ultimately her permanent partner – to understand how she might tend to sabotage their relationship and for them to avoid falling into the trap that she unintentionally set for them.

Emily also helped her partner to see that he too has an orgasm fantasy that affects his behavior even if he is unaware of it, and how together they need to overcome whatever difficulty it may cause for him. Meanwhile, Emily keeps reminding herself that, beyond the powerful feeling of pleasure it brings, the moment of sexual climax is actually a moment of self-discovery in which she attains a profound understanding of an important element of her personality.

Emily undertook this process on her own without the aid of a therapist. One can only admire her ability to acknowledge her problems and examine them fearlessly.

2. Beautiful Women Strolling on the Beach

L iam, a high school history teacher, tells his male therapist that he generally has nice, pleasant dreams about loves, successes and so on (unfortunately, we won't see many cases like this). In his fantasy, he pictures beautiful women strolling on the beach, slim and shapely girls in bikinis, and at this moment he orgasms. In the conscious third level of thinking, however, he is known as a critical person.

A new, rather selfish and pushy teacher started working at his school. She wasted little time trying to rearrange the class schedule to suit her. Liam reacts calmly and pleasantly to her, while other teachers are ready to kill her. "But in staff meetings, I'm known for being highly critical and my friends urge me to restrain myself. I can't abide the idea of students coming to school out of uniform, or smoking, being disruptive and so on. I believe in setting clear boundaries." It wasn't hard for Liam to differentiate between his moderate instinctive responses in personal relationships and his uncompromising, rational criticism at teachers' meetings. The former originated in his orgasm fantasy, the latter in his conscious third level of thinking – just the opposite of his friends, he says. One can well assume that these patterns characterize Liam in general. In an immediate personal interaction, he will be pleasant and easygoing, as in his sexual fantasy. But on the organizational level, with tasks and assignments that have to be completed and that do not involve personal interactions, he is highly critical both of others and of himself. We are probably all familiar with people like this who can be kind and accepting in a personal encounter and abrasive and disapproving in a formal setting (I can think of a few politicians that fit this description). Since Liam's dreams are pleasant, he probably has little need to develop a more defensive or aggressive orgasm fantasy. His critical position within the conscious third level of thinking is related to his identification with authority figures.

Liam seems to have grown up in a judgmental environment with which he identified. As we shall see in many instances in which the conscious third level of thinking contradicts the second level of the orgasm fantasy, we can assume that the third level of thinking develops as a response to the second level of the orgasm fantasy. In demonstrating gentleness in the second level of the orgasm fantasy, Liam often feels unprotected, vulnerable and angry. At the appropriate developmental stage (possibly in the second or third year of his life), he most probably developed a conscious third level of thinking that is more critical and aggressive. At the start of the conversation with the therapist, Liam claimed that his pessimistic forecasts at the teachers' meetings usually come true and that a tougher attitude should be taken toward anyone who harms the system. Later, as Liam began to take responsibility for his different levels of thinking, he understood that the way in which he sees things at the different levels is unique to him and does not negate others seeing the same problems differently.

Improving sex and relationships

Liam greatly enjoys his sex life with his girlfriend. When they sleep together, he enjoys picturing beautiful women strolling on the beach and this tranquil image drives him wild. His girlfriend asks if she is also in the picture and he replies with a smile – not always. His girlfriend has an equally interesting fantasy. She imagines that a certain guy whose name she won't reveal has a birthday; she comes to his house and tells him she has a wonderful present for him. When he asks where the present is, Liam's girlfriend replies matter-of-factly: "I'm the present. Do with me whatever you want." During sex, Liam tells his girlfriend what a wonderful gift she is giving this guy: how he unwraps the gift, opens it and penetrates it while she, the gift, surrenders to him completely – and how in another second the guy's pleasure from the gift will put him in ecstasy. Exactly at that moment, his girlfriend climaxes. Meanwhile Liam switches fantasies and returns to his vision of the women strolling on the beach. Now he too achieves total ecstasy.

Liam's girlfriend – as befitting her orgasm fantasy – is a pediatrician known for her compassionate personality. At home, however, she is quite a slob. Liam has a hard time responding forcefully from his conscious third level of thinking when something bothers him. Instead, he responds out of his orgasm fantasy, gently and with consideration. But when his anger over this has built up, he ends up overreacting and harshly criticizing her. Many people find it difficult to vary their responses to people and situations between different levels of thinking, and tend to be fixated at one level. Liam's girlfriend, who is aware of his laid-back orgasm fantasy, often asks him if he is feeling angry at her. In this way she tries to help him express his anger and not let it build up and fester. Liam, for his part, also understands that in her daily life, his girlfriend gives out too many "gifts" and is always worrying about everyone else, and tries to help her moderate this behavior.

3. TOUGH AT FIRST, THEN "GIVING"

Emma used to be hard on different men she met. She would go from practically ignoring them in social situations to subtly mocking them, almost wordlessly, primarily through her facial expressions. This was in fact a clear sign – which took her time to recognize and acknowledge – that afterward she would "give herself" to them. Of course, many guys were scared off from the start and didn't try to get closer to her, but anyone who did would find that beneath the initial hard outer shell was a profound gentleness and primarily a cry for help. Her boyfriend related dreams of his in which he had to save her: She would be drowning in the sea and he races to her aid, or she would be hurt in a car accident and he rushes her to the hospital. It often happens that our dreams are inspired by the signals we pick up from the other person. How did this tendency of hers to display hardness and then fragility develop? All we know is what the boyfriend recounted. For example, they were once sitting in the kitchen with her father who raised her. In a despairing tone, the father asked the boyfriend: "Why don't you marry her? She's such a good woman, and she's a good cook; it would be good for you" and so on, he continued pleading. For the boyfriend, the humiliation he felt for his girlfriend was nearly unbearable. What happens to a girl who grows up with such a father? Perhaps she tries to protect what little she has until that falls apart too. We don't quite know what her orgasm fantasy was. But her behavior is consistent with sadomasochistic relationships in which she demonstrates toughness in order to instigate conflict followed by total surrender.

At some stage her father was hospitalized. She wanted him to get the best possible treatment and asked to speak to the head of the department. He was busy. When this doctor finally gave her a few minutes of his time, he patted her hand and tried to reassure her. She told her boyfriend that if sleeping with the department head was what it took, she would do it for her father. Clearly, this fantasy was hers – we know nothing about the doctor. Once, Emma's boyfriend asked her whom she would rather sleep with – a policeman or a professor. Her answer was unhesitating – a policeman.

How is a masochistic experience created in a one-year-old child? What causes her to enjoy being berated and suffering? The father who raised her wasn't necessarily a bad father. He seemed to care about her very much. But it's sufficient for the parent to have a hidden sadistic streak in order for a masochistic pattern to develop in the child. The father gives the baby a bottle to drink. She doesn't want it. He forces her.

Just a little, not a lot. She drinks for him, suffers for him. Now she and he are satisfied. The father doesn't have the energy to change her diaper right now. She intuits this and stops crying. She is suffering now for her father's sake. It's no wonder that she is ready to sleep with the department head for her father's sake or that she provokes men in order to ultimately surrender to them and satisfy their desires. The more accurate term for this behavior is sadomasochism, because Emma initially provokes men in a sadistic manner in order to satisfy her masochistic desire. The literature is replete with cases in which a patient's orgasm fantasy appears to be masochistic, but on the conscious third level of thinking, they behave sadistically. Did this sadism develop as a response to masochism and a desire to compensate for it? Perhaps it is the opposite and is intended to provoke the other person to achieve a masochistic outcome? Such questions are reminiscent of which came first, the chicken or the egg. In any event, we see here that the orgasm fantasy and the conscious third level of thinking can be closely interconnected.

Emma's masochistic orgasm fantasy naturally could not compensate for her threatened dream world. In her daydreams, however, she was Beyoncé, strutting her stuff in spectacular stage shows, singing and dancing and thrilling the crowd. This short film often ran through her mind, especially following moments of anxiety or humiliation. Thus, when her boyfriend rebuffed her desire to meet, suddenly she was again Beyoncé feeling tremendously empowered observing herself on stage. Here we see how the unconscious first level of thinking and the conscious third level of thinking can be connected. Emma related that often after climaxing she also saw herself starring on stage. Presumably, Emma achieved satisfaction out of some kind of masochistic fantasy, and after having reached orgasm activated her pleasant daydream in order to dispel the humiliation and low self-worth, she felt due to her orgasm fantasy. We can see that in Emma's conscious world – the conscious third level of thinking – grandiose fantasies appear alongside sadistic ones, and the repertoire could be even richer than this. We also see that the conscious third level of thinking could be connected to the unconscious first level of thinking as well as to the second level of the orgasm fantasy.

Emma did in fact achieve personal development in wake of her daydream and became successful in the field of art. Often it is the conscious third level of thinking that compensates for difficulties in the lower levels of thinking. This is the level that is best connected to the complex reality, and the discovery of ambition at this level can definitely lead people with many challenges to positive places.

Often, a sensitive look from the outside can reveal the different levels of thinking of the person we are with. Thus, with his dream world, Emma's boyfriend brought out the tendencies of her dream world as well as the characteristics of her orgasm fantasy and her conscious third level of thinking.

When we are not aware of our orgasm fantasy and that of our partner, not only do we forego the playfulness and richness it offers for enhancing sexual relations, but we also close off part of our personality, which surely detracts from free and creative thinking.

Improving sex and relationships

Emma and her partner had an excellent sex life. He had sadistic tendencies that meshed well with her masochistic tendencies. In their shared fantasy, he forced her to sleep with various men whom he chose for her. He would ask: "Who is the man you'd least like to sleep with?" Thinking it over she chose an older man she worked with who she found disgusting. He would then order her to give herself to him. Emma shouted, "No! No!" and soon afterward she would be moaning with tremendous pleasure and climax with this image in mind. At other times, he would force her in their shared fantasy to sleep with friends or relatives, even children, and the greater the taboo, the greater the pleasure they both seemed to derive. They will never forget how he once forced her in the fantasy to sleep with her brother. Emma refused, and almost fought with him over this. The boyfriend told her she had no choice, and had to do it. He started describing how her brother was penetrating her, and how she was surrendering herself to him, and suddenly submitting to her body's desires. It was hard for Emma to admit that even though she was used to reaching incredible orgasmic heights, breaking the incest taboo brought her to a truly unforgettable climax. Many of us have dreams in which we have sexual relations within the family, but in the – conscious – orgasm fantasy, this is of course much more threatening and therefore repressed. For humans, this may be the most powerful taboo after cannibalism. Thus, for Emma, it brought the ultimate humiliation and the ultimate pleasure.

Clearly, Emma's boyfriend had issues with women and sought to degrade them. His awareness of this tendency, however, and their ability to incorporate it in their sex play helped the boyfriend to control it in his daily life and especially in his relationship with Emma. His aggressive orgasm fantasy would often pop up out of nowhere. For example, on the road, safe within his car that would soon leave the scene, he would loudly curse other drivers. At other times, when he thought someone was trying to take advantage of him, he might respond with impulsive aggression. However, the more they practiced their orgasm fantasies in bed, the more conscious they became of them and the more they could control them. So, when Emma said something to her partner that annoyed him, he was quick to realize how aggressive he was and was able to stop himself from responding angrily as he would have in the past. Emma, meanwhile, was now sufficiently aware to be able to wonder whether she was not reenacting her orgasm fantasy at that moment.

Emma became a manager in the art field. She saw her challenge as setting clear boundaries for her employees without later changing her mind and capitulating. This wasn't easy for her. But she learned to do so and came to be seen as a very kind and considerate boss.

4. BECOMING ONE

30-year-old William tells his female therapist that he can't experience pleasure unless his wife does. He admits that his pleasure is dependent on hers and that when she achieves satisfaction, he feels that he becomes one with her and climaxes directly after she does. If she does not climax, even if he does, it's worth nothing.

How did such a dependent orgasm fantasy develop? William says his mother always offered him suggestions before he thought of them himself. For example, she would say, "You're tired, go to sleep," before he himself sensed this. When William tells his mother that he's not hungry, she still makes him food. Why? She knows he is hungry but doesn't want to bother her. Even when he's debating whether to go with friends to a movie, he'll probably consult her, thinking she knows better than him what he really wants. At the critical time when William's orgasm fantasy developed (more or less during the second year of his life), his mother probably created this type of bond with him which remained unchanged over the years.

She may have nursed him just before he began to feel hungry. When he started to walk, she was always there to catch him just before he fell. By always staying one step ahead of him, she was denying him the possibility to express an independent will. In this way, she encouraged his passivity and the belief that she knows better what's best for him. But William also had powerful angry outbursts that no one, including himself, could understand – after all, he had such a good mother who was always looking out for him...

William began to bring dreams into therapy from his unconscious first level of thinking about horrible creatures that were hiding all over his house. For example, he had dreams about smiling snakes with prominent fangs and scary eyes hiding under his bed. He associated the teeth and the eyes with those of his mother. The creatures were also cunning, "like my mother," he blurted out – "smiling nicely but also able to strike." This encounter with his dream world was shocking for William. At first, he thought he was a bad person, a total ingrate. After everything his mother had sacrificed for him, is this how he feels toward her?! Little by little, he began to understand that his dreams don't lie and, moreover, they are his. In other words, this is what he actually feels toward her even though he doesn't know it. Thanks to this insight, his angry outbursts began to seem more comprehensible to him.

The outbursts, which derived from the conscious third level of thinking, tended to occur when his mother, and later his wife, had not prepared the food he liked or laundered the clothes he wished to wear. He would lose his temper with them as if they had broken an ancient promise. William also had recurrent violent daydreams: how he'd beaten the crap out of a noisy neighbor; how he'd shot friends who foisted a party on him he didn't want. He noticed that these aggressive daydreams did not occur at random moments; rather they would usually run through his head when he felt he hadn't been able to say what was on his mind.

William says that in conversations with his wife, she says what she thinks and he says what he thinks she wants him to say, as in his orgasm fantasy: "I'm afraid to upset her, afraid to be myself." For example, she wants to buy a new outfit; he thinks they don't have the money for that right now. He tries to find a compromise so as not to assert himself. He realizes that he is storing up anger and fears that he'll suddenly lose his temper with her. For William, the second and third levels of thinking are therefore interconnected. But when there's no food at home, his wife is to blame; similarly, when the clothes he wants to wear are not in his closet. Even though he knows that she works as much as he does, he still blames her for every little thing. In situations where he should say something, he is silent and when he should be silent, he speaks. This is how it is with dependency. He complains that she doesn't look after him and, having decided to turn her into his mother, he doesn't tell "his mother" how angry it makes him when she spends money they don't have. In his relationship with his wife, William has therefore repeated his dependent orgasm fantasy along with a conscious third level of thinking that is filled with anger.

In the course of therapy, an interesting development occurred in William's dreams. He began to have dreams about far-away journeys to marvelous places while she – sometimes his mother and sometimes his wife – watched him recede into the distance. This seemed to signal William beginning to practice separation from the mother figure. In another series of dreams, his mother was a patient in a mental hospital. When the doctors explained to him that she was abnormal, William couldn't stop crying. William seemed to be undergoing an unconscious process of mourning that contained a growing recognition of his mother's complicated personality from which he wished to free himself. As these new dreams appeared, William's angry outbursts slowly began to subside as his self-restraint increased.

We thus see that the conscious third level of thinking in which William has angry outbursts is fueled both by the unconscious first level of dreams and the second level of his dependent orgasm fantasy.

Improving sex and relationships

Even though William's dreams changed and his angry outbursts gradually abated, his orgasm fantasy did not change. This is something he will need to develop control over. William's wife tried to encourage him to reach orgasm without her, and even sometimes before her, but without success. She then suggested that he use his imagination to envision her experiencing a powerful orgasm. Sometimes this worked, but needed more practice. Sometimes she would fake orgasms for his sake, and their ability to laugh about William's incredible dependency also helped somewhat. Increasingly, William was able to tell his wife what he wanted and to stand up for himself, and his angry outbursts also became less frequent. When William wants to reach orgasm, he still imagines that his wife is climaxing, and he along with her, but in their marriage, William has become the leader in many areas; lately, in particular, he has taken control over financial matters.

William's wife has an orgasm fantasy in which she sees herself having sex with William in public places: in a car parked in the middle of the street, in the public park, or in her classroom at the university. She imagines a crowd of people watching them in awe. William understands that it's not that his wife actually wants others to see her naked but rather that she has a deep need to feel that she is being seen. In social gatherings, she also tends to seize the limelight and do a lot of the talking. By getting to know his wife's orgasm fantasy, William is better able to accept her.

In bed William describes them having sex in a public park. Passersby are approaching and offering them suggestions how to do it even better. One spectator even wants to show William how to do it right. William's wife says she wants a woman spectator to teach her the best way to do it. Still in the park, laughing, William tells her she must climax before him so that he can join her. His wife, however, wants to hear more reactions from the crowd. William invents several more cries of encouragement and flattering responses from the women. When his wife is sure that she is being seen and that everyone sees her, they see her well, she suddenly begins to climax with intense pleasure and William naturally experiences the same pleasure along with her.

The sex is now over and soon they will both fall asleep. She asks him plaintively: What am I lacking? He caresses her and tells her that he will always see her. For as long as he lives, he promises, he will really see her. She tells him she'd like him to be stronger, more independent, and less dependent. He promises her he will change in other things, but not in bed.

5. I, MYSELF

In Olivia's orgasm she sees another woman masturbating. The next moment she'll say that she is the woman in the fantasy. What is so special about Olivia's orgasm fantasy is that she is watching herself satisfying herself. Even in her body language this is how she behaves. As Olivia, an attractive blonde with striking eyes, walks in to the clinic, she pleases herself with her physical movements. This is what her orgasm fantasy looks like to the therapist, a woman, observing her. Her arms twist with each movement she makes, her head almost seems to be licking her body, and her constant smile or trace of a smile all seem to be directed mainly toward herself. When the therapist says something, Olivia listens closely, then carefully enunciates what the therapist said, phrasing it slightly differently so that she can really absorb it. Usually she doesn't agree or doesn't quite agree even if the therapist repeated something that she, Olivia, had said. It all has to come from her. This behavior also matches her orgasm fantasy of watching herself giving herself pleasure.

We note her writhing body language, her habit of directing her words to herself and the inner-directed smile that implies she is savoring a secret that only she knows. Every orgasm fantasy can be described in physical terms, because its origin lies in the primal parent-child bond. Thus, a person's orgasm fantasy will always be a part of him, wherever he may be.

How did this orgasm fantasy develop? Olivia was raised primarily by her father because her mother was very ill from the time she was very young. When Olivia's father took her to the mall to buy her clothes, they would end up coming home with clothes for him instead. What happened to Olivia's clothes? She tells her therapist she doesn't really know. She just remembers that often when she would start to tell him something about herself, the subject would quickly change to him. Her father expected her to be a top student and refused to accept any talk of difficulty. "It's not really hard for you," he would tell her with a gleam of admiration in his eye. Olivia did indeed excel in school. At the same time, she had to listen to him talk about his problems at work and help him in many other ways, again because her mother was unable to play this role. At school she was often ostracized by the other children. Olivia notes insightfully that this was because she was simply egocentric. The therapist winces: "Pain upon pain," she says to her. "First you were egocentric because you didn't have enough for yourself, and then when you tried to care for yourself, you were punished." Olivia started to cry.

Thus, from very early in life, Olivia didn't feel she could rely on her father to really see her. And so this intelligent child developed satisfying and comforting imaginary scenarios.

Perhaps she pictured that she was playing by herself in the many hours that she was left on her own; or maybe she learned – as many children whose parents don't pay attention to them do – to keep herself busy. So when she stimulates herself, she feels satisfied, which is exactly what happened.

Olivia's dreams fall into two clear categories. In one, she is alone, with no other people around her. If other people do appear, they are far away and unreachable. Sometimes they come closer but do not speak, and in particular do not look at her. The image seems to be dark and she has the sense that in the dream she is depressed. She makes no attempt to change her fate, but just endures the dream by herself. The second type of dream, more optimistic but also more infrequent, is about wishes. For example, she dreamed that her father phoned her and then she woke up to another disappointing morning; she dreamed that she and her mother were going out somewhere, something that hadn't happened in years. Much later, Olivia learned to understand the significance of the two types of dreams: how an elusive feeling of optimism she hadn't dared to think of would suddenly sneak into the dream, while, for the most part, she is engaged in repressing the moments of loneliness.

Compensation for the above, however, is provided by Olivia's daydreams: Here she is a member of parliament who changes the world, especially in the field of education. She builds special preschools that teach creative thinking, transforms abandoned children into successful adults, etc. In a more recent daydream, she advances the cause of world peace by brokering a peace treaty between hostile African countries. Over the years these daydreams were Olivia's most closely guarded secret. "Maybe even more than my strange orgasm fantasy," she says. "I was so embarrassed to tell anyone about them." "Why?" the therapist asks. Olivia ponders: "This desire to be someone, that's what's so embarrassing." "Why?" the therapist asks again. Olivia considers. She doesn't really know. "Maybe because in this daydream I'm telling other people that I'm better than they are. Maybe because it's condescending." "But you're helping the world in this daydream," the therapist persists. "Yes," she says, "but it's still condescending." Olivia says she's noticed that this daydream recurs whenever she expects someone to pay attention to her and it doesn't happen. In the past, this often occurred when she waited in vain for her parents to take more of an interest in her and to notice her academic achievements. Today it happens when someone disappoints her, then suddenly she's a famous member of parliament who is busy bringing about world peace. At night she knows that she will feel lonely but right now she's a powerful lawmaker. Her therapist says that maybe if Olivia hadn't seen that spark of admiration in her father's eyes, she wouldn't now be picturing herself as such a powerful figure. Olivia agrees that she did at least get something good from him – her daydreams and the ability to fulfill them, as she proved in her studies.

Improving sex and relationships

Olivia "forgot" to tell her therapist that she has a boyfriend. For several months, she spoke only about herself and hardly ever mentioned him. The therapist reminded her of her orgasm fantasy, which could be the reason she is so focused on herself. Olivia finds it hard to climax when her boyfriend is inside her, which bothers her. After he climaxes, she wants him to leave her alone for a while; she then masturbates and climaxes. She also doesn't want him to watch her in these moments. As far as she's concerned, it's best for him to turn around and look the other way. Olivia's boyfriend loves her and understands how she is trying to reclaim what she never received from her parents. This helps him overcome his feeling of insult, both in their sex life which is not very satisfying for him, and in her never bothering to ask him if he wants anything when she goes to the supermarket. When Olivia asks him in wonder why he loves her, he replies simply – "Because I get you."

Lately the couple's sex life has improved. The boyfriend penetrates Olivia and doesn't move, which is what she wants. Without him disturbing her she can masturbate by gently rubbing her clitoris engrossed in her orgasm fantasy. She then climaxes. The boyfriend needs a few more minutes of intercourse and climaxes as well. Only recently has Olivia realized that she doesn't know what he's thinking about when he climaxes, and asked him. He imagines a scene in which she is begging him to sleep with her. When she is really pleading and telling him how badly she wants it – this is the moment he suddenly comes.

These days Olivia also asks her boyfriend what he wants when she goes to the supermarket. She also understands that he needs her to be less immersed in herself and more appreciative of him, as evidenced in his orgasm fantasy. Lately, before going to bed she begs him to have sex with her. But she also understands that he needs to feel this admiring and appreciative attitude at other times of the day as well.

6. TEAR ME APART

35-year-old Oliver says that he gets the most pleasure when a girl says to him: "Tear me apart, put it in as strong as you can, I'm opening everything to you." Oliver wants to describe this very precisely: "I can imagine that the girl is saying all these things to me. But if she actually says it then it's definitely better. Without her permission, however, whether in reality or in my fantasy, if I'm just acting on my own, it doesn't turn me on. That is, I need her permission to let my anger out and feel pleasure." Again, we see that it is often necessary to explore the orgasm fantasy in detail in order to understand the complexity of the experience. Unfortunately, we have no information about Oliver's dreams or his conscious third level of thinking.

Oliver says that his current girlfriend plays along nicely with the idea. His problem is that it's the same for him in his daily life: He has to ask permission from the other person in order to say what he wants, to find self-fulfillment, and to assert himself. For example, in his marketing job he has many interesting ideas about how to boost sales. He feels certain that his ideas would help but he won't argue with his superior. He'll barely ask permission to finish presenting his ideas. For the most part, he'll wait to be invited to share his ideas, just as in his orgasm fantasy. The other people on the marketing team walk freely into the boss's office, make suggestions and try to promote their ideas, while he "walks on eggshells" and waits for approval. Listening closely to Oliver's orgasm fantasy, however, reveals other elements. Not everyone needs approval from his girlfriend for his aggression, perhaps because not everyone is so filled with aggression. When talking with his friends, if they allow him, he dominates the conversation and goes on forever complaining about different people who have done him wrong and what a cruel and messed-up world we live in. He carries on at a furious pace and doesn't let anyone get a word in. Oliver needs others' approval and attention in order to express his pent-up anger. Whenever he feels that the other person isn't fully listening – which is what usually happens in life – he'll find it difficult to speak his mind and will keep his anger to himself.

Where does Oliver's tremendous anger come from? What took place between the infant Oliver and his mother who cared for him that made him so angry? And why will he only express this anger when she approves and not when he wants to? Let us imagine that Oliver wants to nurse. His mother might be busy at the time and unavailable for him. His anger starts to build up. If he gets too angry and begins screaming, she might get upset and frustrated. Or she may simply ignore him as happened before. Possibly she'll also get angry with him and purposely refuse to come to him. His mother may be a good woman but she needs her quiet and can't tolerate being forced to do something. Finally, she comes to nurse him at a time that suits her more than it suits him. She smiles, he's furious and crying and possibly hitting out. She smiles again, understanding him and allowing him to let his anger out. Little Oliver understands that he can vent his anger only when his mother is ready, when she is with him, calmer, and can handle it. An orgasm fantasy thus arises that contains tremendous anger that may only be released with the other person's approval.

Improving sex and relationships

Oliver's girlfriend has no trouble telling him how much she wants him to "tear her apart." She loves him so much, she says, that she is glad to totally submit to his fantasy. And what is her orgasm fantasy? Oliver once asked her if she would be willing to sleep with someone in his department so that the guy would let Oliver have his excellent class notes to study from. She didn't rule it out. Oliver told her right away that he was just kidding. But the girlfriend kept on wondering about the notes for a long time. She seemed ready to do anything for Oliver. Moreover, it seemed that this was exactly her fantasy – i.e., she was ready to do this but for her own sake.

Oliver's girlfriend's orgasm fantasy might be that she climaxes when she feels she is helping someone else or possibly even sacrificing herself for someone else. There are apparently many people like this. Oliver, meanwhile, liked to give her little tests now and again: Once when they were driving, a cop pulled them over and gave them a ticket for a traffic violation. When they drove off, Oliver asked her if she would be willing to sleep with the cop in order to get the ticket canceled. She thought about it, smiled and said – Why not? Oliver didn't stop there. During sex with the cop would she be willing to do whatever pleased the cop most, to ask him what his orgasm fantasy is and to fulfill it. This time Oliver's girlfriend smiled even more. She doesn't know what the cop's orgasm fantasy would be, but if they're already having sex, she says, then why shouldn't he enjoy it? Oliver knows he has found a goodhearted woman and he loves her for this. And she loves him because he lets her be a part of him and fulfill his fantasies. Some would say that his girlfriend has no personality of her own. But she would reply that it is precisely this personality of hers that makes her, and others, happy.

Some time later, enjoying a good meal in a restaurant with a glass of red wine and talking about their fantasies, Oliver's girlfriend admits that her orgasm fantasy, like every orgasm fantasy, has certain disadvantages. Oliver nods in agreement; he knows what she is talking about.

7. ONLY I'M ALLOWED TO COME

Charlotte has an orgasm fantasy in which she is lying on a table surrounded by serious businessmen engaged in discussion. Every so often, someone comes to have sex with her and leaves a few bills by her side. This impulsive girl obtained great pleasure from sex. She does not seem to feel exploited; on the contrary, in her sexual fantasies she feels flattered by being narcissistically in the center. She asked her boyfriend to tie her up and do whatever he wants with her. This request did not come from a masochistic stance but rather from the pleasure of knowing that she is important, central and vital. Again, we see that the overt story doesn't always depict the hidden emotion that needs to be explored, and that the same story can have different emotional meaning for different people. Once, during sex, she surprised her boyfriend by suggesting that he invite his friend in the next room to join the party. Here too, she would be at the center. Another time, she excitedly related how she saw a weary soldier at a hitchhiking station, called out to him and then invited him to sleep with her, "just like that, so he would feel good." For her, this was a gesture of strength. But her narcissism had other less positive aspects as well. She could sit in the classroom on the first day of university studies, look around, not recognize anyone and immediately say that everyone there was stupid and that she wouldn't carry on studying in that department. It was that difficult for her to give someone else room, to understand that not everyone is stupid, and that she might learn something from the professor.

In romantic relationships, she displayed hysterical tendencies. If the boyfriend expressed doubts about their relationship, her level of hysteria soared. When he wanted to end the relationship, she would chase after him, preventing him from leaving, and just couldn't tolerate rejection. At times she would act as if she was being unfaithful – suggestively embracing another guy while the boyfriend looked on in envy. Sometimes, she actually did cheat on him, claiming that she was not responsible for her actions, but rather had been led by her emotions: "What could I do?! It's what I felt." Another time, during an argument she asked him to perform oral sex on her. She climaxed but then refused to let him have intercourse with her so that he too could obtain satisfaction.

Charlotte had a warm and admiring relationship with her father, as opposed to power struggles and mutual wariness with her mother. She would describe her mother's manipulations, how she always knew what her mother was aiming at, and that she, Charlotte, wouldn't fall into her trap. "Take a sweater, it's cold outside," the mother would say. But Charlotte knew that her mother wasn't really worried about her, but rather about her self-image as a mother, and therefore wouldn't take the sweater. But the real "victory" over her mother probably began when she was just one or two years old and still in the playpen. What was the nature of the relationship between Charlotte and her mother that dictated the development of such an orgasm fantasy? Probably already then, the mother was looking at little Charlotte in expectation, awaiting whatever she might say. Not so different from those businessmen in her orgasm fantasy who are longing for her.

One can see Charlotte in the playpen, smiling. Her mother is busy and Charlotte is making noises, wanting attention. Her mother says, "I'm coming in a minute." Charlotte isn't ready to wait. Her mother apparently caused her to be unable to wait. She already gave in many times before. Now Charlotte is screaming. She knows that this will upset her mother and that she will capitulate. Precisely at this moment the baby feels as if her mother is sitting inside her head, ready to fulfill her wishes as if they were a single entity named Charlotte. In this way Charlotte develops a narcissistic mindset in which she is at the center and most important, is unable to see the other and to delay gratification. Later she will tend to look for such a relationship with her partner.

What about Charlotte's positive relationship with her father? This seems to have contributed to her conscious third level of thinking. Here Charlotte could be part of a saner and more moderate world and tell her boyfriend how much she appreciates his kindness and his honesty – directly after enacting dramatic scenes from her orgasm fantasy in which she drives her boyfriend mad with jealousy. Thus, through interaction with reality, each level of thinking can be independent and develop separately. Sometimes, however, an interesting connection takes place between the different levels. We don't know anything about Charlotte's dream world, but her appearance strongly projects a feeling of restlessness: protruding lips, eyes racing in their sockets, fluttery hands and a suspicious look in the corner of her eye. Her narcissistic orgasm fantasy seems to help her compensate for the powerful feelings of rejection from her inner world.

Improving sex and relationships

Charlotte and her boyfriend broke up. Charlotte's responsibility for the breakup is clear, namely her narcissism and inability to see the other. She also failed to make a connection between her orgasm fantasy and her day-to-day behavior. Her boyfriend, however, also contributed to the failure of the relationship. In his orgasm fantasy he watched a strong, handsome man sleeping with his girlfriend. At his girlfriend's moment of climax, as her arms and legs are flailing with tremendous excitement with the man leaning over her, he experiences a powerful orgasm. A closer examination of the boyfriend's orgasm fantasy does not reveal homosexual tendencies or a wish to be entertained. Rather, he wanted a strange man to sleep with his girlfriend in his presence because in his mind he felt he was too small and too weak for such actions – like the little boy who imagines his parents having sex that he is not a part of, or a boy who leaves the stage to his big father. At his girlfriend's moment of climax, therefore, the boyfriend, in addition to a powerful orgasm, also feels deep humiliation. It pains him that he is not the one who is satisfying her. When Charlotte cheated on him, he was deeply hurt but, strangely, also wanted her to tell him every little detail about the sexual experience. Charlotte felt that this clearly aroused him sexually while at the same time being emotionally painful for him.

With an orgasm fantasy such as this – and especially with him being unaware of its significance in terms of his relationship with Charlotte – he was unable to provide Charlotte the security that could have reassured her. Being constantly hurt naturally reinforces vulnerability. Later, Charlotte will marry another man who will provide her with stability. When a couple is not getting along, it is recommended to examine their different levels of thinking, which might deepen their understanding as well as provide a solution. In this case, the conscious third level of thinking does not seem to have been the problem for either of them (she could compliment him for being a good guy and apparently, he really was a good guy). But an examination of their orgasm fantasies could at least have helped them to understand the dynamics of the situation and why they were both so unhappy in the relationship.

8. Can Trust Be Sexually Arousing?

James, a kind young man who likes to help others, tells his therapist that he has unpleasant dreams in which he tries to do various things but for some reason they never work out. Others, however, are more successful than him. James does not project confidence, and comes across as introverted and hesitant. He is rather scrawny, breathes haltingly and often seems to be shivering. In his orgasm fantasy he is undressing a woman. "What do you mean exactly?" the therapist asks, knowing that the details of every orgasm fantasy should be carefully examined as they often reveal hidden truths about the patient's experience. "What's the mood like and what is happening between the two of you?" he continues. James says that in his imagination, the girl trusts him fully and this is what arouses him. He envisions himself slowly undoing the buttons of her dress. She is standing there, he says, very still, with a little smile on her lips. She is relaxed and accepting.

She knows that she can trust him and so waits quietly and patiently. And then… in the middle of observing this patience or maybe the middle of undoing a button or seeing her smile, he suddenly comes. No, he doesn't need to undo many buttons; he just has to do it very slowly and when he recognizes the trusting look, she gives him, he celebrates his triumph.

James also built relationships of trust with other people based on a similar type of experience to that he envisioned undressing his girlfriend. He is a very honest and non-manipulative person who expects the same treatment from others. However, if someone lies to him or betrays his trust, he cannot get angry with or confront that person. Rather, he tends to say to himself, "He's not worth my anger. There's no point revealing to him how I feel," and he then breaks off contact. James also describes how hard it is for him to negotiate his pay at work. He always tends to say what he really thinks and won't try to negotiate based on what he believes he could obtain from the other side. His friends tell him that he's being a sucker.

One girl who happened to hear about James' orgasm fantasy, said, "What a sweetie!" How then does such an orgasm fantasy about trust develop? James' mother apparently instilled in him the feeling that she trusts and believes in him. This is accomplished by listening to him, to his crying, to his complaints, and believing that he must want something genuine, that he's not simply crying for no reason. But many mothers act in this way, enabling their babies to internalize the kind look from their mothers who respect their wishes as if they were adults. He sees that she believes in him, and that she is there for him. How can one describe from the outside the internal experience of trust that develops in a baby? In this case, James was the first of his classmates whose mother explained the mechanics of sex to him. This was in an era when sex education was only whispered about and not taught as part of the school curriculum. James once told his religious parents that he didn't believe in God. This time, it was he who felt safe enough to put his trust in them. On another occasion, young James was given a chocolate bar by his mother. She suggested that he share it with his friend standing next to him. Little James refused. His mother did not scold him or snatch away the chocolate. She respected her son's wish even though it was rather egocentric and certainly not socially acceptable. All she did was to let her disappointment show on her face. She gave the friend a piece of chocolate from somewhere else. To return, we can imagine little James in the playpen gazing at his kind mother and seeing something in her eyes that will be etched in his mind forever in the form of an orgasm fantasy that is all about trust.

On the conscious third level of thinking, James has a recurring daydream in which he is saving people and being showered with admiration. In one version, a plane makes an emergency landing and James directs the passengers to a safe escape. The reader might not find this to be particularly moving, but James has tears in his eyes whenever he envisions this scene. Does James run this film through his mind whenever he unconsciously – i.e., from the first level of thinking – feels guilty? Possibly. As we have said, the three levels are interconnected and trigger each other. Like many people, James tends to actualize his daydream in his daily life. He is known for his kindness and for being helpful to others. He can go overboard with this as well, as in his tendency to go on and on explaining something he is knowledgeable about to the point where the person who asked the question is sorry they ever brought it up.

What type of dynamic develops between the different layers of James's thinking? As we have seen, James has a tendency toward anxiety in the unconscious first level of thinking. He builds trust relationships in the second level of thinking, in his orgasm fantasy. And in the conscious third level of thinking, he rescues people in his daydreams. But where is the anger? Where is the assertiveness or aggression that we don't find in any level of thinking in James's emotional world? When people don't express their anger, it is repressed and, as we know, is transformed into depression and anxiety, which is what characterizes James's inner world. His orgasm fantasy – building a trust relationship – which is his developmental solution to the depression and anxiety, doesn't always work. In life, one sometimes has to know how to be aggressive as well. Becoming familiar with his orgasm fantasy will help James to sketch the differences between himself and others and to gain deeper insight through his recurring fantasy that while giving trust is his "default" behavior, other possibilities exist, such as being assertive. This is James's "absent fantasy" that he will have to work on developing either on his own or in therapy.

We will often speak in this book about "the absent fantasy." As the name implies, this is a fantasy that is not present, or only very weakly present in any of the individual's three levels of thinking. As a result, this fantasy is less familiar to the person and it is harder for him to make use of it. For James, the absent fantasy is assertiveness. In other cases, we will meet people who have difficulty feeling guilt, others who are unable to admire anyone – including themselves, of course – and so on.

It appears to be easier to direct a person to act from a different level of thinking in which the necessary attitude exists, rather than to invent this from scratch when the tendency is absent. For example, we can help a person not to act from the automatic default response of his violent orgasm fantasy, but rather to respond in a way that is more thoughtful and forgiving if that is present in his conscious third level of thinking. Sometimes the opposite is true, and we would like him to act from his orgasm fantasy in order to encourage him to be more spontaneous and authentic. When a certain type of attitude barely exists in the person's emotional world, we try to teach the person how to engage this "absent fantasy", the assumption being that all types of feeling are accessible for everyone.

Improving sex and relationships

James wants to look his girlfriend in the eye and see the trust she feels as he enters her. He doesn't imagine penetration at all, but rather how he slowly undresses her as she smiles tenderly at him. Meanwhile, she fantasizes that the apartment is spic and span, with everything in its proper place, just where she wants it: the papers are neatly stacked, the clothes are folded, the cushions are nicely arranged on the couch. This is the moment when she comes. He wants tenderness and she wants control. We see here that the orgasm fantasy doesn't necessarily have to be about sex, but can be simply a certain kind of emotional expression. Usually when James and his girlfriend have sex, they are absorbed in their own fantasy world, but sometimes one of them will come out of their shell and tell the other the fantasy that he or she would like to hear. So, James will tell his girlfriend how clean and neat their apartment is, just the way she likes it. Then she'll ask him, "And what about the floor?" And he'll say that he vacuumed and mopped it, and it's really shiny, and then she just needs to add a little more from her own imagination about how the house is completely in her control and … then it happens. Or she will smile at him, thrust out her chest and ask him to undress her. Inside, she's laughing, but this body language and these words have their effect on James and it doesn't take him much more to reach orgasm.

In everyday life, however, things are more difficult. James's girlfriend is in a quandary: How can she help him become more assertive? Should she really tell him not to give in to her, which is what he usually does? She tries but it's not easy for her. Then she sometimes lets out her mean side, as she says, and intentionally tries to get him mad. She wants to see him angry, which happens only very rarely. James, meanwhile, recognizes her need for control. The orgasm fantasy is not only about house cleaning; James's girlfriend tries to control him as well as her colleagues at work. So, in those moments when she is telling James what to wear and how to eat, he looks at her lovingly and quietly tells her that she is now speaking to him out of her orgasm fantasy.

James thinks that he and his girlfriend, despite awareness of their fantasies, have not changed very much. Mostly, they have learned to accept themselves and each other. This is the big change they have made, which would not have happened without them being conscious of their orgasm fantasies.

9. Do It Just the Way I Like It

Sophia is a forty-year-old attractive woman with charming dark curls and big blue eyes. For years she has been chasing a married man who has yet to keep his promise to leave his wife. In her daydreams, they live together and have a wonderful family of their own. She knows exactly what their house will look like and pictures how they will each leave for work in the morning, and return in the evening. Other men who want her she rejects with contempt. "I'm a bitch," she says. "I'll go out with a guy without taking my wallet, let him lick me but stop him as soon as I'm satisfied, not respond to his texts and then post something on Facebook just to make him jealous."

In the conscious third level of thinking, we can say that Sophia has a pleasant daydream about her warm relationship with her married man. This pleasant daydream probably kicks in at moments of disappointment and despair that Sophia's mind is trying to fix for her. Again, he hasn't replied to her message, again he doesn't have time for her, and then suddenly in her daydream they're living together happily ever after. In moments like these, the disappointment is repressed into the unconscious, into the first level of thinking – dreams. But why is Sophia so disdainful of other men who want her?

It seems that Sophia is responding to them from deep within her orgasm fantasy. "My last boyfriend would lick me in the most amazing way, with love, and really listen to me, just how I like it. But it basically doesn't matter to me who it is." Indeed, in Sophia's orgasm fantasy, she is in the center, the most important person in the world, receiving all the attention, and no one else exists. With such a fantasy it's not surprising that she responds in this way when she is not interested in someone. Did Sophia's mother behave this way with her during a critical period in early childhood? Most probably.

"According to the family stories, my mother was a good mother, very warm and nurturing until I was about three. I'm told that I was her whole world and that she hovered around me constantly - running to me for every little thing. Then my younger brother was born and I lost my special status as an only child. In those years, my mother also started working and was much less available for me. I remember being a whiny and restless girl. To this day my mother doesn't understand me. When I want to tell her something, she immediately switches to talking about herself and about how she raised me and my two little brothers amid many hardships. She never even calls me these days. My father, on the other hand, was more affectionate but he was hardly ever home." Sophia's female therapist wonders if Sophia's mother was once warm and involved, or possibly submissive to little Sophia's desires, which could explain Sophia's tendency to erase others.

Sophia indeed seems to be reenacting with this married man her ceaseless running after her mother when she was a child, trying to regain the lost paradise in which her mother belonged solely to her, really saw her and was invested in her as if no one else existed. This scenario can be seen as an outgrowth of the conscious third level of thinking. However, when someone does not conform with this desirable scenario, she relates to them from a regressive and more automatic position of the second level of thinking – from her egocentric orgasm fantasy in which she is the center of the world and others serve her in the way she experienced her mother's relationship to her in her earliest years. The contrast in Sophia's personality is intriguing: in her orgasm fantasy she seeks only to receive, while in her daydreams she is prepared to give everything to her married man. It is not unusual for the connections between the second and third levels of thinking, which here are simply an age-old reenactment of Sophia's development, to appear this way.

Sophia has two main dream themes, the first a painful insight that reveals her failure, and the second a pleasant experience of wish fulfillment. In the first she is singing in a choral ensemble but can't keep the right pitch and keeps going off-key. The other members of the choir turn around uneasily. Her associations with the dream quickly led her to say that her married man likes to sing and sings well: "So maybe we're not good together." Thanks to the dream, she is able to say something she was unable to say in the many hours she spent daydreaming about their home together. In another dream she wanders the streets of an unknown city at night, trying to find her way but not succeeding. Here too, the dream helped her admit to herself that she was in a trap with her married man that she can't get out of.

In the pleasant dream theme, church bells are ringing and she, a young girl with braids, is still sleeping. A man comes up to her, kisses her and whispers in her ear that they need to hurry to a wedding. This is how I experience myself, she tells her therapist – as a little girl. In another dream she and another man are in the kitchen preparing a meal together, a wonderful experience, she says.

It seems to Sophia that in those moments during the day when she has clear insight and realizes that nothing will come of the relationship with her married man, suddenly at night they are together on the couch. And just when she is having pleasant fantasies about their life together, the dreams come and upend the entire situation. Such is the world of dreams, certainly not prophetic, but simply the missing pieces of the emotional puzzle that have been repressed.

Improving sex and relationships

Sophia doesn't need to improve her sex life. She can easily reach orgasm by fantasizing that a man is performing cunnilingus on her. She is also very open to her married man's sexual desires and their sex life is flourishing. But Sophia needs to learn not to be so egocentric with men as in her orgasm fantasy, and also not to negate herself and only serve the other person as she tends to do in her conscious third level of thinking with her married man. Sophia fluctuates between the two thinking levels that represent contrasting fantasies, and has not been able to find the balance between them.

Recently Sophia managed to break up with her married man. She subsequently met this "nerdy" guy, as she describes him, and says "he's not a man and doesn't know how to really have sex." He is one of those men she was bitchy to in the past and couldn't even think of bringing into her bed. She tells her therapist she knows that if they sleep together, she'll stop being bitchy with him, lose her power over him and start running after him. "Maybe that's why you demean him," the therapist suggested, "so that he won't demean you." This makes sense to Sophia. Sophia then slept with her nerd and said it was the best sex she'd ever had, which she attributes to the fact that he was open, wanted to hear her orgasm fantasy and put it into practice. This so-called nerd loves Sophia's sexual openness, and with him she feels that she can also realize her daydream of a home and family. The deep conversations they have are helping Sophia to gradually understand that neither one of them has to be demeaned.

What is interesting here is that sexual relations changed Sophia's response to her boyfriend from the second level of her bitchy orgasm fantasy to the conscious third level of her daydream about closeness. In case study No. 3, Tough at first, then "giving", we saw how Emma followed the same path but in the opposite direction. She would be tough on guys she met from the third conscious level of thinking and after they slept together, she submitted to them through the second level of her orgasm fantasy. In this way sex can reduce conflicts and promote closeness. Sex seems to facilitate a transition between different levels of thinking, or, within the same conscious third level of thinking, a transition to a gentler and closer relationship.

The boyfriend told Sophia that in his orgasm fantasy he is going down on himself, sucking himself. "Yes, in the fantasy I can reach there," he responds to her astonishment with a smile. But Sophia is a sensitive woman. In bed she can tell him how he is sucking himself, or she can suck him while telling him to imagine he is doing it to himself, while at the same time she understands how much loneliness there is in this fantasy. Sophia's boyfriend often acts as if he doesn't need anyone. He is more than willing to assist other people but finds it hard to ask for help. It's as if he can't believe it could happen. Sophia says that when she looks at his cold and aloof parents, she is not surprised. Now in bed when she holds him in a maternal embrace, he tells her that his mother never hugged him that way and only with her he doesn't feel alone.

10. FUNNY SEX

Even though it took her a while in therapy to be able to say this, Elizabeth says that she doesn't know who she is. She has this image in her mind of a hollow head that can be filled with anything, and imagines different people she meets tossing all sorts of stuff in there. Elizabeth switched boyfriends frequently. She fell in love with all of them and thought she would marry them because they were just right for her – until the moment that everything blew up. But when she is helping others, everything feels different. She remembers herself in kindergarten as the good girl who always helped everyone: soothing a child who was crying, giving another child crayons to calm him down, and taking all the struggling kids under her wing. She still remembers how her kindergarten teacher would send her to calm all the kids who were crying because their parents had "abandoned" them at school. Now when she tells her female therapist this story, just the memory of it makes her emotional and she feels the "high" of someone who finally knows who she is. "I'm like a primitive woman who lives for others," she adds in a moment of insight, even though Elizabeth is a university lecturer.

Indeed, in the conscious third level of thinking, Elizabeth adapts herself to others. She behaved in this self-negating way with the men she fell in love with until, inevitably, things fell apart.

What does the dream world look like of someone who doesn't know who she is? Elizabeth had many dreams in which she was not herself. Once she was a little Gypsy girl with braids who was playing in the neighborhood. Another time she was a black cat that belonged to a very nasty family of cats with sharp claws. At other times she is part of a bunch of hippies and has five children. Her dreams, with their changing roles that she assumes and discards, depict far better the feeling of not knowing herself than any verbal description. While we may all appear in different guises in our dream world, if someone only rarely appears in his real identity, this is indicative of the distance he feels from his true self. We may therefore presume that there are more "costumes" in children's dreams because their separation process has yet to be completed and their self has not yet crystallized, while adults will tend to see their own selves in their dreams.

A child knows who he is when he can see himself reflected in his parents' eyes. But if there is no parent who will tell him in a thousand ways and reflections who he is, how will he know? Think of a person growing up without a mirror – how will he know what he looks like? Elizabeth's mother and father were her friends from when she was very young but weren't her parents. The baby Elizabeth thus failed to derive the benefits of the first unconscious level of thinking, the dream level, but was able to gain more as she got a little older and the second level of thinking – her orgasm fantasy – began to take shape. In her first year of life when Elizabeth needed physical contact and a warm and close connection with her parents, they weren't there for her. They were the sort of parents who feel helpless with a baby who needs acceptance and closeness and doesn't understand what is being said. Later, in her second year of life when she began to speak, the house was filled with humor and laughter.

The therapist observes how charming and playful Elizabeth is, quick to laugh and always with a twinkle in her eye, and how enjoyable she is to be with. She knows, however, that Elizabeth's orgasm fantasy is "working overtime" with her as well. What most arouses her, Elizabeth tells her therapist, is joking and kidding around with her partner and laughing during sex. It's no wonder that so many people love her even though she doesn't love herself that much.

Did this laughter that was imprinted in Elizabeth's orgasm fantasy compensate for the inner feeling of emptiness in her unconscious first level of thinking? It probably did. In the conscious third level of thinking, however, Elizabeth feels sorry for her parents and has been concerned about them from the time she was young. After all, as we saw in her behavior at the kindergarten, this is how she finds meaning. Later we learn that Elizabeth sought therapy because she was constantly angry, which was causing her problems with her colleagues and students. When Elizabeth negates herself in the unconscious first level of thinking and doesn't know who she is, it's inevitable that anger should arise in her conscious third level of thinking. Her friends disagree about her "problem". Some say it's her insecurity while others say she's too aggressive sometimes. Who is correct? All of them it seems. On the unconscious first level of thinking she is insecure, doesn't know who she is, and frequently changes costumes, while on the conscious third level of thinking she can be aggressive and angry, or as we have seen, helpful and compassionate. But "in the middle," in her orgasm fantasy with the automatic behavior that derives from it, everyone loves her and her laughter.

The therapist observes Elizabeth and points out that Elizabeth has never been angry with her. People often connect with others at one level of thinking and not another. Elizabeth doesn't want to be angry with her therapist; she wants to laugh with her and be loved by her. Sometimes the therapist feels very confused about her, a common situation with people who don't know who they are. When Elizabeth leaves the room, the therapist asks herself what exactly they talked about and finds it hard to pinpoint.

Recently Elizabeth began appearing more often as herself in her dreams. For her son's birthday, this was the first time she didn't stay up all night working on a beautifully decorated poster, and the first time she didn't spend hours running between shops to find him the Superman shirt he most loves. She had a much more modest birthday celebration with him and felt much less angry at him. Her laughter-filled orgasm fantasy was the only thing that didn't change...

Improving sex and relationships

Elizabeth's husband finds things difficult with her. He also doesn't know who she is. Sometimes she feels sorry for him, at other times she's angry and often – spontaneously – she's laughing and full of fun. In truth, he is unaware that he doesn't know who she is. He simply feels that she is unpredictable. This is what happens when you live with someone who doesn't know who she is. He prefers her to be angry with him rather than feeling sorry for him. That way he knows that she is expressing on her conscious third level of thinking something that is missing in her, and not some fake identity.

Familiarity with each other's orgasm fantasy is very important for a couple, but often it is just as important to get to know the main tendencies of each other's other two levels of thinking. All these together comprise the personality and make sense of things. In Elizabeth's case the problem lies in her conscious third level of thinking, her anger, not on the second level of her orgasm fantasy. When this is in operation, everyone loves her.

Elizabeth is not looking for love and romance during sex. She wants the kind of laughter one has among friends. Her husband, however, does want romance and love, and doesn't want to turn sex into one big joke. In his orgasm fantasy, they are a pair of lovers at sunset. He pictures the two of them watching the sun go down… gradually sinking closer to the water… any moment now it will touch it… Exactly that moment of contact is when he comes. Elizabeth's husband has trouble believing that other people have different fantasies. All the beautiful travel posters show couples at sunset. Elizabeth still finds it funny how gently he treats his colleagues at work on the basis of his sunset model, while he finds it silly the way she makes a joke out of everything.

What's funny about sex? Once when he was having difficulty penetrating, he said to her: "What don't you understand?" She replied in astonishment: "Don't you think it's funny how you're trying so hard to put it in and then once you've succeeded you'll have to take it out, and then the whole thing just keeps repeating itself. But it's more than that. I enjoy laughing with you, when we're laughing together it really turns me on." He then told her he had a fantasy in which she was lying in bed and he showed up at the door naked, wearing just a tie, with a nice black hat atop his erect organ. Astounded, Elizabeth asks him why he never told her about this wonderful fantasy and that she wants him to do it for her right now. He immediately leaped out of bed and a minute later came back to the room just like that, with the tie and hat. Elizabeth started laughing hysterically. The husband penetrated her easily with Elizabeth still laughing and suddenly climaxing.

They lie side by side, exhausted, and she asks him, "What kind of man acts like such a romantic?" "And what kind of woman makes a joke out of sex? It's usually men who do that," he retorts. Now that they both understand that it's okay sometimes to switch roles and enjoy it, they feel that they love each other even more. He asks, "Why do you get so angry with me sometimes?" She replies that it happens at moments when she doesn't know who she is or what she wants. He asks how he can help. She says she has to think about it but that he's already helping her just by having this conversation.

11. RIDE ME

Jacob dreamed he was driving a fancy car and accidently hit a pedestrian. He panics, flees the scene, and hides out in some yard feeling terribly guilty. In the clinic he recalls how, the evening prior to the dream he hurt his mother's feelings by finally letting out his anger at her for always pitying him and belittling him (we have here a good example of the associative work of the dream; hurting his mother was translated into hurting a pedestrian). Jacob has many guilt-related dreams in which he gets into trouble and runs away. Another theme of his dreams concerns his dog to which he is very attached. In these dreams the dog is taken away from him and he barely protests. He simply gives in, cries about it and mourns. In one dream he saw someone else walking in the street with the dog. The dog gazed at Jacob sadly, as did he, but again he didn't do anything. Even though Jacob's parents threatened several times to give the dog away, he knows they won't. Nonetheless, he often dreams about how they are separated and that he doesn't put up a struggle.

With dreams like these, one wonders how Jacob behaves in his daily life? He has dreams of guilt and grief but these are just feelings and not reality. So, we must turn to Jacob's orgasm fantasy. In the first version of his fantasy, a woman with large breasts is lying on top of him and clutching him to her. He shows his female therapist how the woman presses his shoulders close to her. From his description, the woman is clearly pitying him. Then he comes. When exactly? At the peak moment of pity and togetherness. A few months later, Jacob says he has found a more arousing fantasy. He is lying on his back while she sits on his chest. Then, at the moment he is at his most submissive, he comes. Jacob and his therapist understand that the default option in Jacob's behavior is not that the woman should pity him but that she should dominate him. Thus, through a lengthy and careful examination process, often in stages, one can come to identify his or her orgasm fantasy.

Will Jacob now reenact this kind of relationship with the whole world? Jacob admits how difficult it is for him to look people in the eye and say hello. This is how submissiveness operates. However, if Jacob's conscious third level of thinking were more optimistic, perhaps help could come from there.

Unfortunately for Jacob and his therapist, his third level of thinking is no more successful or optimistic. He constantly hears a refrain repeating itself in his head: "I'm a loser." Sometimes it's "I'm worthless," at other times, "I'll fail for sure." He can't avoid these words coming to him at the most inopportune times – when he wants to concentrate on a paper he has to hand in at the university or when a test is handed out, or when he wants to start up with a new girl. Jacob has been depressed for years. The three levels all cooperate with depressing thoughts that mutually reinforce each other.

Both as a child and as an adult, Jacob does not express aggression toward his parents or anyone else. In a rare childhood incident he threw a vase of flowers out the window, for which he received a stinging slap on the face from his father. Since then his aggression has ceased. Without a minimal amount of aggression directed outward, we would probably all be in an inwardly directed depression.

Jacob's parents, who themselves have depressive tendencies, were never particularly enthusiastic about anything he did. Whenever he tried to do something new, to enroll in a new department in the university, or to try his hand at a new type of art, his parents would say, "Why bother? You'll only fail again and get depressed." Apparently, this is how his conscious third level of thinking – "I'm a loser" – was shaped. He simply internalized what his parents kept telling him throughout his childhood, whether in words, body language, or facial expressions.

Jacob needs his girlfriend just as much as he needs his therapist, and runs to them whenever the depression surges and the "I'm a loser" voices reverberate in his head. Thanks to them, he can calm down for a few hours until the voices reappear. He clearly invites others not only to calm him and tell him what to do, but primarily to control him. At these moments his orgasm fantasy switches into action. Is this the way his parents controlled him when he was a baby? Even now, as an adult, he still shares all his little aches and pains with his mother so that she can tell him what to do. But why does a baby want to be controlled? Surely in order to achieve bonding and love. So, the baby adapts himself to his parents. He tries to meet their emotional needs, perhaps their need for control that will extricate them from their depression. Jacob says he even has trouble giving commands to his dog; he feels as if it controls him.

Not all Jacob's dreams are about guilt and mourning. Fortunately, he occasionally has more optimistic dreams. There is a difference between people who are depressed in their everyday life but find a ray of light in their dreams, and people who are depressed during the day and again in their dreams. The situation of the latter appears to be worse. Such people need to adopt qualities of joy and optimism that don't exist in their world, while the former need only to shift the balance and become more aware of themselves.

Jacob's therapist understands that the missing fantasy in all of Jacob's three levels of thinking is his ability to be assertive towards the world. She knows that assertiveness and even aggression will give him a feeling that he has power and that he is worthy, and will lessen his depression in which he attacks himself.

Another fantasy that Jacob lacks is admiration. When his therapist makes an admiring comment, Jacob is very excited. But he just isn't able to admire himself. He needs it to come first from the outside, like all of us. But luckily for Jacob and his therapist, there are many reasons to admire Jacob, some of which

THE ORGASM FANTASY • 59

the therapist reminds him about at every session: his sensitivity, kindness and impressive creativity in various areas. Aggression and admiration, admiration and aggression – these are the things that the therapist needs to work on with Jacob (his absent fantasies). The therapist deliberately uses the word "aggression" rather than "assertiveness." She would like to see Jacob being aggressive, the rationale being that only a genuine release of his impulses will extricate him from the depression. Politely standing up for himself just won't be enough. As we know, the orgasm fantasy does not change throughout life. Dreams and conscious thinking can change slowly and incrementally, but need to be enriched with new experiences. Lately, Jacob has been having a dream about disconnecting from his cable supplier, called YES; to say NO to YES, in other words to start speaking up for himself and standing his ground.

Only recently has Jacob's therapist realized that the way he enters the clinic, hunched over and confused as if he were searching for something on the floor, is a reenactment of his orgasm fantasy. They will have to work on this as well.

Improving sex and relationships

Despite his depression, Jacob is a very sought-after guy. What do girls see in him and depressive types like him? Perhaps it's the sensitivity and gentleness that is lacking in the average macho male. Jacob is a great writer and painter and a wonderful dancer. So why wouldn't a girl fall for him?!

Jacob goes through many girls and is quite a heartbreaker. How does he do this? He looks for a girl who will breathe some joy into him and not be drawn into his depression. He tells her about his orgasm fantasy, how she is sitting naked her legs spread on his neck, forcing him to go down on her. At the peak moment of submission, when he is trying so hard to fulfill what he imagined to be her wish in the best way possible – that is the moment when he comes. The girls want to cheer Jacob up, and comply with all his desires. Afterward, they switch roles. Every girl has a different wish. By now, Jacob is used to fulfilling all kinds of the girls' strange wishes. Recently, for example, he had a girlfriend who could only climax when she imagined that she was having sex with children. Jacob reassured her, explaining that this was just a fantasy and she shouldn't be alarmed by it. "There are no handcuffs on thoughts and imagination," he tells her. Yes, pedophilic material is outlawed because it encourages actually taking such photographs. But in the imagination everything is permitted, or, as Jacob tells her, not only is it permitted, it is desirable. These images exist within you whether you want them to or not, so it's better that you control them consciously rather than repressing them into the unconscious where they will control you. This girl will subsequently claim that Jacob helped her more than any therapist to accept herself and to have a normal life even with these "perverted" fantasies.

But Jacob is never the one to initiate a breakup with a girl. Rather, he just makes their life miserable with his misery and tells them every morning how he's such a loser, until they can't take it any more.

Jacob is depressed, so it's not surprising that he has problems getting an erection. And the anti-depressants he takes surely don't help matters. He feels he has to explain to girls the first time they sleep together why he has trouble getting it up. They think that it's somehow because of them. He simply asks them to let him quietly start fantasizing, then he sits the girl down on his chest – only in his imagination this time, and now she is forcing him… And suddenly he sees that he has an erection, that he is penetrating her. Jacob says the orgasm fantasy is better than a thousand Viagra pills. He thinks that if people would simply discover their orgasm fantasy, the companies that manufacture all the chemicals to induce erections would go bankrupt.

Jacob tells his therapist that it's not easy the first time he's with a girl to talk to her about his orgasm fantasy. But this kind of talking does create a bond and a feeling of trust that the girls find thrilling and they are up for every challenge. Then he tells them what a loser he is and they tell him that he's the greatest guy they've ever met.

Jacob continues to paint romantic pictures and to write beautiful poetry, and not to vent aggression. "In fucking there is aggression," his therapist says, trying a more direct approach. "An erection is the symbol of the aggression. What is penetrating someone else's body if not aggression? There is no fucking without aggression," she tries again. "Why do people yell at one another, 'Fuck you'? Not out of love, but out of hate. Look at animals and you'll understand what this natural aggression is that you are lacking. Jacob, you have to learn to be aggressive, otherwise you won't be able to fuck."

The therapist could not have been any cruder. But in Jacob's orgasm fantasy, he is the object of the aggression and not the aggressor. He is the one being controlled, not the one in control. Jacob's therapist has come to realize that one doesn't have to be aggressive in order to fuck. You can also be the object of the aggression – this is what arouses Jacob. The therapist is finally forced to admit, just to herself of course, that she was actually expressing her own passive orgasm fantasy, expecting some degree of aggression from the man. Every therapist needs to be aware of his or her own inclinations and not project them onto the patient (countertransference in professional parlance).

Jacob has had many girlfriends. He doesn't choose them on the basis of their orgasm fantasy, but rather according to their conscious third level of thinking. He wants girls who are happy. Whoever wants a relationship with Jacob must get to know the three levels of his fantasy. She'll have her work cut out for her, but it will be worth the effort.

12. PISTONS GOING UP AND DOWN

In her unconscious first level of thinking Evelyn has a wide variety of dreams. Two themes, however, seem to predominate. In the first, she touches people and they cease to exist. Sometimes they dissolve, sometimes they crumble into pieces, and sometimes they become distorted beyond recognition. Evelyn recalls the legend of King Midas in which everything he touched turned to gold, and how miserable he was because of it. She thinks that for her it's even worse. Was Evelyn unable to touch her parents? To reach them? Did they disappear every time she tried? Evelyn agrees with this description. Her father wasn't there for her and her mother was helpless. Possibly this is why she sometimes sees her mother's internal organs in her dreams. Evelyn doesn't know how it is for others. She only knows that she doesn't know how to form a relationship.

In the other series of dreams, Evelyn is having sex with her father and her brothers, and once, even with her mother. In her dreams she has already slept with friends, both male and female, with children and old people and practically everyone she knows. What could be going on with Evelyn such that her relations with almost everyone are translated in her unconscious into sex? She says that in this kind of relationship it is clear what you give and what you receive. In real relationships, she adds, all of this is unclear. Was there sexual abuse in her childhood home? She doesn't think so. But she does think there was a lot of sexuality in the air.

When she comes for therapy, she admits she feels like someone who goes to a prostitute. "Why?" her female therapist asks. "Because I'm paying for you to listen to me and pay attention to me. Isn't this what people go to prostitutes for?" "I thought that you come here for a genuine relationship with me?" the therapist challenges her. "How can it be genuine if I'm paying for it?" Evelyn answers. She feels sure that a relationship is purchased with money or sex and that you usually don't get what you want. She also knows from her dreams that a relationship usually ends in humiliation – when she is the one who disappears.

Evelyn is an attractive young woman who entices men to sleep with her. More than once they have told her that this is ruining their relationship, that she should wait a while, it will come. But it's hard for her to wait; she wants a relationship now.

Evelyn's difficulty in forming a relationship is most noticeable to the therapist at the end of a session when it's time to leave the clinic. This is a moment when patients usually turn to her, make eye contact, smile, offer a word of thanks, or some gesture. But with Evelyn there is none of this. She turns her back to the therapist and leaves. The therapist draws Evelyn's attention to this, saying that it seems to be hard for her to separate, and that she expects her to turn around and stop for a moment. Evelyn acknowledges that it is terribly awkward for her. Later they practiced these goodbyes at the end of each session. Evelyn joked that it would make a good movie. The therapist told her that it's okay to feel awkward, and that this is also an important part of every relationship.

Recently Evelyn dreamed that she gave birth to twins and they were taken away from her. Someone from the welfare services came and explained to her nicely that she is incapable of being a mother and will only harm her children. Evelyn did not argue or protest; she remained silent and felt that this was the correct thing to do. She also remembers watching the woman go away with the children while she stood there feeling she knew that this would happen.

When Evelyn was very young, her mother abandoned her and went off to India to find herself. Her father had bouts of depression, and when he wasn't depressed, he would start a new business, only to fail and become depressed again. To this day, Evelyn feels that her mother is not there for her. And she feels so sorry for her father. Evelyn adds many more details to her childhood story: how her mother never called her to come home in the evenings when she'd been out playing in the neighborhood; how she was always the last one left outside; and how her father spent years not leaving his bed or speaking to anyone. But even as this information piles up, the therapist feels that she still doesn't really understand Evelyn's inner experience. Clearly this experience cannot be understood from the outside, and only the patient's three levels of thinking pave the way for penetrating this enchanted world.

Evelyn doesn't think she has orgasm fantasies. After the session she went home, talked about it with friends who shared some amazing stories with her, and she did some homework. She undressed, sprawled out on the bed, spread her legs and began to masturbate. Suddenly she saw body parts moving toward each other, penises like pistons going up and down, penetrating again and again, plus a few bits of thigh and some stomach, but nothing else. The body parts machine kept working at a steady pace, and the machine was clearly satisfied. She wondered why this image suddenly appeared as it had never done so previously when she masturbated. She thinks that the therapist's instructions helped her to be less restrained. Perhaps her friends also helped. The well-oiled pistons continue their smooth motion and suddenly… she sees stars, or maybe fireworks, followed by relaxation. The machine disappears. Evelyn, however, knows that henceforth the machine will come back whenever she masturbates, possibly for the rest of her life. This what her therapist told her. Maybe it won't be a piston but something else that tells her story – a relationship that isn't personal, but rather one that's like a machine.

Even though it seems like the wisdom of hindsight, the therapist has the feeling that she already knew in some way about Evelyn's orgasm fantasy, namely that Evelyn has an orgasm fantasy without a human relationship, a fantasy featuring only body parts, not human beings.

What does Evelyn think about during the day? What is her conscious third level of thinking? "I'm very good at tasks and organization," she says. "Very efficient. My days consist of composing neat lists of tasks." Despite this, she tells her therapist how easily she is distracted – how one thought suddenly jumps to another and then she can't remember what she was originally thinking about. When two levels of thinking – the second and third in this case – are characterized by a similar feeling, it usually points to the dominance of that feeling in the person's world. In Evelyn's second and third levels of thinking, however, there is no feeling.

Evelyn quit therapy fairly soon. She felt that the therapist wasn't there for her, wasn't really with her. Apparently, she too disappeared when Evelyn tried to touch her.

Improving sex and relationships

Evelyn has never had a long-term romantic relationship. We can only imagine how her first encounter with a potential boyfriend might develop. Evelyn is an intelligent woman. She will inquire about the guy's orgasm fantasy and be ready to immediately play the role that his fantasy requires. The guy will love this, and will then probably offer to fulfill her fantasy. Evelyn may be a bit embarrassed to reveal her fantasy which seems so strange to her. Eventually she'll overcome her embarrassment and the guy will demonstrate to her how the machine works. He will begin slowly and gently and then increase the pace. Evelyn will correct him and tell him that the emphasis in the working of this machine is not its strength; rather, it's a delicate machine that works more gently. But it's still a machine without a human connection. The guy will slow the pace and concentrate on the penises, trying to read her thoughts. Evelyn lifts her head to watch the machine, she sees their thighs spreading and converging, sees the piston, and suddenly she is coming apart along with the machine. No machine could continue functioning at such a level of pleasure.

Having achieved satisfaction, she has a strong feeling of emptiness. She wants a relationship, and any relationship is better than none at all. The kind boyfriend will try to caress and hold her and give her what her parents deprived her of. If he is affectionate enough, it might work. Suddenly at night he's not so quick to vanish or crumble before her eyes. Her dreams may gradually change as well. Suddenly she might not dream that they are sleeping together. The boyfriend may be insulted – why others but not him? Evelyn will explain that he is different and this is what's so good about him. He offers her what she has never had, a relationship. Suddenly not only in a dream but in reality, too, Evelyn won't want to sleep with him. By now she doesn't need sex for a relationship. She wants him as a loving father. But Evelyn is intelligent enough to realize that there is no conflict between the two things; perhaps the opposite. They will love each other more if they have sex and it is good. During sex, she, of course, can picture whatever sort of machine she wants, just not a loving father – which would preclude any possibility of pleasure.

In her daily life or in her conscious third level of thinking, Evelyn will become less detached, and will no longer need to keep running errands as a means of escape. She will allow herself to feel how her friends leave her alone and she won't have to dream about people who disappear. Everything is now under the control of the conscious third level of thinking and not freely running wild as in the unconscious. All of this can happen if Evelyn becomes aware of her three levels of thinking.

13. The Surprise...

Janet has a hard time with her husband, but in bed things are great. She never stops reminding him that in bed she's the boss, and out of bed, she adds with a chuckle, she's often the boss as well. This is exactly what the orgasm fantasy teaches us, namely how we revive our orgasm fantasy relations in automatic everyday behavior. She can come to him suddenly, grab his penis, pull his pants down and go down on him. Then she pushes him onto the bed and starts to ride him. Janet's husband likes to lie there passively and let her do the work. All he needs is suddenly to come. He seems to like such surprises, to come when he's not ready for it. He says his wife brings out good things in him. Janet says she is most aroused when she surprises him, and can only come when she sees the stunned look on his face.

Her female therapist asks if she has daydreams. Janet ponders for a moment and recalls how she sometimes pictures herself impressing tall muscular men. They meet for a date and with her attractive appearance and quick-witted tongue she captures them in her net. Janet says these men remind her of her father with whom she still struggles endlessly. Indeed, Janet is a control freak. In her second and third thinking levels, she wants to be in control, which leads to constant conflicts with her husband who also wants to be in control, if not in bed then on the ground.

She wants to control her therapist as well. She either doesn't show up, or she's late; she decides when the session will start, if at all. She often keeps important things from her therapist, another way of controlling the therapy and what the therapist knows about her. Recently, Janet admitted that she isn't even sure she wants to make progress in therapy. She will decide whether her therapist will be successful or not. Later, a deeper truth emerged. Janet is aware that any progress in therapy will hasten the end, and she doesn't want to have to part from her therapist. This leads to Janet's surprising dream world.

In her unconscious first level of thinking, as expressed in many of her dreams, she meets good-looking guys and flirts with them. All of a sudden, she notices that her husband is also present. Once he appears in the shape of a cat who watches her, and sometimes she just recognizes his shadow. Even when she meets in a dream with her parents whom her husband doesn't like, he's suddenly standing at her side.

Janet jokingly protests to her therapist that even in her dreams she has no privacy. How come her husband is present in all the dreams where she is doing things he might not like? The reason is obvious. If during the day Janet sees a man who attracts her, she then thinks of her husband and what he might do if she were to cross the line. She therefore immediately represses the thought to her unconscious and it reappears in a dream. Indeed, even in her thoughts Janet cannot be alone. To be more precise, she is the one who will not allow herself to be alone. Not everyone who imagines cheating immediately places his or her partner in the picture. Janet has many other dreams about dependence. In one recent dream, she was a little penguin trailing after a big penguin that was running away from her.

The therapist thinks that were it not for Janet's dreams, she would never have imagined what a dependent personality was hiding within this pretty and vivacious girl. And how in her conscious world, the two higher levels of thinking, the controlled person becomes the controller in order to repair her inner experience.

Janet's relationship with her parents is filled with discord, even hatred. What happened in her earliest childhood and onward that shaped her second and third levels of thinking with a need for control? Janet surely tried to free herself from this primal dream world and apparently also from a reality of severe dependence on her parents with the aim of gaining control over her life. Did she actually gain the upper hand over her parents throughout her childhood in the many struggles between them in the way she imagines in her fantasies of control from her second and third levels of thinking? Apparently, she did succeed, and even if not always, this was her aim. In her mind, relinquishing control was akin to plunging into an abyss of enslavement, helplessness and being subject to others' control, something she would never let happen.

Janet describes the following scenario with her husband: She wants to go out to meet a girlfriend but thinks her husband wouldn't want to be left alone. She asks him if she can go. He tells her it's okay for her to go. However, Janet senses that her husband doesn't really want her to go, and would prefer her to stay with him. She tells him she feels that he wants her to stay and that she is ready to forgo the meeting with her friend. Her husband repeats that she can go. "No, I won't go," she says first to herself and then to her husband. "You don't really want me to go." Janet did not go to see her friend.

Is Janet controlling or controlled? Is she dependent on someone else or is someone else dependent on her? Her therapist thinks that Janet is an example of how domineeringness and dependence are two sides of the same coin. She says to Janet: "First you get into your husband's head and constantly try to adapt yourself to him. This is your dependent side. But you also constantly control him: You think you know better than him what he wants and what's good for him." Janet's therapist thinks that this is a beautiful example of a dialogue that encompasses the universal truth of how domineeringness and being controlled can be intertwined in a person's psyche, and how one aspect may not be able to exist without the other.

The therapist is waiting for Janet who doesn't arrive. Is Janet controlling her therapist or is she controlled by being incapable of ending therapy which she misses more than she attends. Only Janet's three levels of thinking can make this clear to Janet and her therapist, and without exploring these, Janet will never understand who she really is.

Improving sex and relationships

Janet and her husband don't require proof that their orgasm fantasies play a part in their everyday lives. They both recognize Janet's impulsivity and her husband's tendency toward passivity. She is like fire, he'll say, and she'll say that he is like water – quiet and calm. But when she rides him, which he enjoys and is grateful for, she asks him not to be so hurt by the way she also "rapes" him in their everyday life. She knows she is raping him at not one but at two levels, and that it is not easy for her to change this. But she asks him to love her the way she is and to remember how much she needs him and how much she is really dependent on him. He tells her that she reminds him of "the weeping rapist" who rapes women and cries at the same time, and that what he enjoys in bed is demeaning to him in life which is why he constantly feels a need to fight with her.

Later they talked about how she would moderate the rape a little and do it in a more pleasant manner. And he would resist the rape, as anyone would be expected to do, but he wouldn't really resist completely. He then tells her that if she wants to sleep with another man, he could help her. It doesn't matter that much to him. He loves her and cares for her and just wants her to be happy. She smiles a bit skeptically; he may not totally believe himself either. She thinks that if in her dreams she would also feel that he is helping her and advising her with men rather than standing there like a menacing shadow, she would love him so much more. But they both appreciate that some dreams tell a story that they themselves cannot tell, and that in dreams it is not possible to lie. He says there are people who are offended by their partners' dreams, or even hide them from each other, and they both laugh…

14. NO EYES

30-year-old Mason makes life very trying for his family. He slams doors, doesn't answer when spoken to and complains that others don't answer him. Mason was diagnosed on the autistic spectrum with Asperger's. He is talented in various areas, good-looking, has a fine sense of humor and can also easily laugh at himself. So why doesn't he do something with these qualities, his frustrated female therapist wonders. One can talk to him about anything, but nothing changes. Mason has been stuck in the same box for years, without friends, male or female. Mason agrees with everything his therapist says to him; he truly does agree and is not just saying so. In other words, he really does understand, but as has been said, mental hospitals accommodate many people who have marvelous insights about themselves and the world but remain there nonetheless. Understanding, therefore, is only part of the story.

In Mason's conscious third level of thinking, he does not have any orderly daydreams, but as we have seen he does have a lot of anger that he vents on his family. Will Mason's orgasm fantasy provide any insight into why he is like this?

When Mason masturbates, he says that he sees a woman. The sex is maybe a little technical but the woman seems to be enjoying it. But and this is the big but, Mason complains that the woman has no eyes. "What do you mean," Mason's therapist presses him. Mason says that her eyes are blurred, in his imagination of course. This evidently bothers Mason, otherwise he wouldn't complain about it. Are eyes a sign of connection? This is what we understand intuitively at least, as well as from the psychological analysis of drawings. A connection is made with the face, the facial expressions and mainly the eyes. Mason knows that his orgasm fantasy will not change but in therapy he is still fighting to change his fate.

Will the first level of thinking, Mason's dream world, shed light on his problem? What kind of dreams is a person with Asperger's who is detached from his surroundings and has no relationships outside his family likely to have? It's not hard to guess. All Mason's dreams are about his family, which implies that his inner experience is focused on them. He sees them in his imagination, thinks about them, and seems to have no space or freedom for other people. This would explain why he is not forming connections with friends even though for several years his therapist has been encouraging him to do so. Once, for example, he dreamed that his whole family was vacationing on a yacht at sea. He gazes with binoculars at the horizon and sees storm clouds approaching. The others are relaxed and laughing and he is the only one who sees this. He immediately revs up the engine to full force and steers the

yacht toward the nearest island. On the day preceding the
dream, Mason was worried about the massive rain clouds and
feared that their house wouldn't be able to withstand the storm
and would be flooded. When he warned his parents they hardly
reacted. In another dream, he saw a huge lizard in his room.
He yelled to his mother for help but she didn't respond. Mason
would say that this is what his mother is really like. When he
says something to her, she might only reply a few minutes
later, absorbed as she is in her own thoughts. She doesn't try to
bond with him. And his father? In Mason's dreams, he always
appears in profile. No eyes looking at him, nor any smile. Once
he dreamed that his father was a flat shadow that knocked
on the door of his room, and then without waiting for an
answer, slipped in under the door. Mason went over to him and
accidentally stepped on the shadow and felt terribly guilty. It
reminded him of the shadow of Peter Pan that got lost and so
Wendy sewed it to his shoe. Mason says this is how his father
is: lacking independence like a shadow, always the opposite
of him, or in relation to him, never saying anything clearly,
never really himself. When his father wants the window closed
he'll ask for it to be opened because he thinks his request
will surely bother someone; when he feels guilty that he's not
involving Mason in the planning of a trip, he'll accuse him of
not having offered; and when he sees that Mason is miserable
and friendless, he will blame himself. What happens to a
child who grows up with parents like this? Perhaps in his
imagination he looks for eyes but never finds them.

Mason possibly teaches us something important about the
inner world of babies. At the start of life, we are naturally

focused on our family, and the baby dreams about his parents because this is what he knows. But already at this stage, in his first year of life, Mason's mother was not emotionally available to him and his father even less so. Hence the dreams. In an attempt to solve the riddle of his existence, Mason is unconsciously preoccupied only with them and the unsatisfying relationship he has with them. Then, in the second year of Mason's life in which his orgasm fantasy is shaped, he doesn't see eyes, which can probably be explained by the fact that his parents who look after him are unclear and their behavior is very confusing. Mason creates an orgasm experience that does not have a real bond. And not long afterwards, in his conscious third level of thinking, Mason starts to accumulate anger and resentment that only emerges about twenty years later.

When the therapist asks Mason why he doesn't try to start a relationship with girls or try to make friends, he says he just doesn't believe that he can do it. For him, it's inconceivable that anyone would ever say "yes" to him. How does such a feeling arise in a person? His therapist has told him countless times that he is handsome and talented and the day will come when girls fall at his feet and then Mason will beat himself up for all the years he wasted. None of this convinces him. He knows that he will fail at forming a relationship Why? Simply because his mother doesn't answer and his father has no eyes.

Improving sex and relationships

Mason has never slept with a woman, nor has he ever gone on a date. He obviously needs somebody active who will initiate and take him under her wing, so to speak. She will understand his difficulties and he, being very intelligent, will respond to hers. Mason, who does not see eyes in his orgasm fantasy, needs a girl who will see him, who will convey clear messages to him, and not confuse him like his mother and father.

He needs a woman who dreams about the wider world and not only about family, who sees in her dreams figures who create a connection and not profiles that lack expression and a voice. It would be best if her orgasm fantasy did not involve technical sex and that she would not, for example, see body parts (as we have seen previously). It doesn't really matter what her orgasm fantasy is; the important thing is for there to be a relationship between the figures. And in the conscious third level of thinking? As we've said, motivation to form a relationship will suffice. She won't regret it.

We see how sexuality hitches a ride on the imprinting of our first relations with the figures who care for us. Apparently, sexuality needs the most powerful vehicle – our default response – in order to be realized.

Mason's therapist decided to do something unorthodox, to take him out of the clinic and introduce him to a girl. Why is this usually regarded as unacceptable? Who said it's forbidden? "Maybe it's my conservative education," Mason's therapist thought to herself.

THE ORGASM FANTASY • 81

The three of them sat in a quiet café. Why quiet? Because that's what suits Mason's personality. The therapist immediately took a step back and the couple talked. Mason was afraid he wouldn't have anything to talk about. He really does need someone who will take an interest in him. That way he will also learn to take an interest in her. He needs a girl who isn't put off by her boyfriend's passive tendency but recognizes his hidden strengths. Mason does ask questions and show an interest, but something is missing, the therapist realizes. He always asks her after she asks him, but never initiates. "So, don't I interest you?" she asks, offended. Mason is a good student and will quickly learn how to show interest, to take responsibility. He just needs the right woman to teach him.

Later they went to bed together and here Mason was not passive, but "technically" even a little violent and angry. The girl looks Mason in the eye and asks him if he sees eyes; she wants him to come while he is staring deep into her eyes. But she doesn't understand that Mason's blindness is internal and not external: he sees eyes but doesn't feel that he sees them. It would be easy to dominate Mason but Mason needs a girl who doesn't dominate him; he's had enough of that at home. He needs a girl who is like his therapist, which is hard to find. Every so often the girl asks him what he's thinking, what he's feeling and what he wants. Mason will reply with honesty and total openness, as long as she is the one taking the initiative and asking the questions. "Mason, every morning, ask me…" she has taught him. And he has learned. Indeed, everything can be taught and learned. Mason proves this. He just needed a good teacher.

15. The Exhibitionist

Maya is in therapy because she cheats on her husband at night in her dreams. In one dream she was talking to her lover in a pub; he wasn't really listening and was looking elsewhere. In another dream she was waiting for him on a dark street corner and he didn't show up. And in yet another she saw him walking on a bridge connected to the end of the world, hand in hand with another woman. Maya stood under the bridge and breathlessly watched them disappear into the red horizon.

People often come for therapy following a marital crisis brought about by an affair. They may also seek therapy because in their dreams they are having fun with various lovers and they realize they are longing for another relationship. Maya, however, comes for therapy because even in her dreams she is unable to create a satisfying relationship. The inner world of someone who is able to be unfaithful in her dreams is different from that of people like Maya who are unable to follow the cheating to its logical conclusion. The former is able to conceive of another relationship in which she is loved and desired, something that Maya wants but cannot fulfil. Maya's male therapist grasps the intensity of her loneliness, thinking that were Maya able to fully realize her nocturnal cheating in the course of therapy it would constitute a successful outcome.

Despite her dreams, Maya is a strong and successful person in real life. It could thus be beneficial to examine her defenses against the inner experience of emptiness and desolation. The defenses belong to her conscious third level of thinking – her daydreams about the end of the world.

She knows how the end of the world will look, how the earth suddenly splits in two and maybe shatters into more pieces. At that moment she is standing on her balcony gazing at the view that is disappearing right before her eyes, along with her. In another daydream, the sky is all red and she dives into this vast expanse. In these moments she feels no fear, but rather a sense of excitement, possibly even a pleasant feeling. Why would a girl and then a grown woman invent such scenes in her mind?

Her therapist suspects that for Maya the end of the world is preferable to her nightly sense of abandonment. Maya thinks that everyone is equal at the end of the world. Besides, the end of the world is beautiful in an eerie way. The conscious third level of thinking thus transforms the abandonment and fear from the first level of thinking into something beautiful. Such are the wonders of the healthy mind that produces bold inventions in order to defend itself against pain. At some point

Maya tells her therapist that she heard that the last wish of astronauts whose spaceship had malfunctioned, dooming them to fly through space for eternity, was to be buried on earth.

But Maya has another compensation for her lonely nocturnal world – her orgasm fantasy that she takes everywhere and which makes everyone love her.

Maya comes into the clinic with a slow, calculated walk, as if she were in a fashion show. Smiling, she makes her way slowly to the armchair. The therapist feels he has to admire her, which he does because Maya is a very attractive woman. Often, she will stop for a moment in the center of the room, and only when she knows that she has been observed will she casually take her seat. What could be the orgasm fantasy of someone like Maya who enters a room this way?

Ever since she was a little girl Maya has had a fantasy that really arouses her. She is in her childhood bedroom, slowly getting undressed. The windows are wide open, she is almost naked, and knows that some unknown person is watching her. She removes her underwear, the observer watches, and as she goes to the window, she feels a powerful thrill. As a teenager, she says, this thrill became a sexual climax. Some patients are aware of their orgasm fantasy even in pre-adolescence.

One can assume that Maya managed to dispel her loneliness from the unconscious first level of thinking by means of an orgasm fantasy in which her mother sees her. It is her mother who is the watcher at the window, the one for whom she has to put on a full show. Now it is her therapist. Presumably there was something good in Maya's relationship with her mother. Through its survival instincts the baby knows how to build a bond with the caregiver parent that will suit them both. In Maya's case, she caused her mother to admire her body and today Maya is the one who admires herself and adds others to this circle of admiration. But what happens when nobody admires her or when her husband who loves her is incapable of providing her with the admiration she seeks? Then the unconscious erupts painfully from the first level of thinking into the conscious third level of thinking, which is why Maya seeks therapy. She tells her therapist about her strong feelings of emptiness and lack of meaning, which her therapist understands as conscious expressions of third-level thinking for the unconscious feelings from first-level thinking. She needs someone to listen to her, wait for her, and hold her hand until the end of the world – all as in her dreams.

Maya does well in admission interviews for university and in job interviews. She makes a good impression wherever she goes and also evokes in her therapist a feeling of responsibility and love for her. In a certain sense, our personal orgasm fantasy is a part of our fate, not something we have chosen, but something that may certainly determine our future.

Maya tells her therapist about other thoughts from her conscious third level of thinking, feminist theories that she has wholeheartedly embraced. Why feminism, the therapist wonders to himself? Perhaps because of the pain? Perhaps the rejection? It's not easy for a male therapist to hear feminist theories that constantly put men down. Even though he feels an urge to defend them, his desire to protect Maya is stronger. He hints to her that it may be related to her unconscious pain, that she shouldn't exaggerate and hate all men because there are some who are nice. "Like you, for example," she says, and for a moment this fills him with contentment.

Maya tells her therapist she believes that many feminists have masochistic orgasm fantasies, and that by means of their conscious third level of thinking in which they are rebellious feminists, they try to compensate for these fantasies and to come out looking strong. "How do you know?" he asks her. "Isn't it obvious?" she replies.

Maya's therapy should continue, her therapist tells her, until at least in her dreams she is able to obtain what she wants.

Improving sex and relationships

Maya wants her husband to peep at her surreptitiously. How should this be played out in bed? He has to stare at her and study her naked body, she says, smiling, but not as he is doing. He has to stare as if she doesn't notice. She looks to the side, he continues to study her body, then finally gets up and hides behind the curtain and peeks toward the bed. "That's not it," she says angrily. "You don't understand! Not like that!" "How?" he asks, almost insulted. Then she stands naked in the middle of the room, looking to the side, and he caresses her body with his eyes. She likes this a little more. Maya understands that such tricks won't really help her. She has to work with her fertile imagination to which nothing can compare. Then, during intercourse, Maya is somewhere in her childhood bedroom with the huge, wide-open windows, slowly stripping.

Someone is observing her, perhaps with binoculars; her body feels him, she knows he is there. But she has to ignore it, keep going as if she is totally unaware, as if she has an unspoken agreement with someone she has never met. Suddenly she gets up the courage and stands completely naked in front of the open window. A cool breeze caresses her as he stares at her totally exposed body. Later she won't remember what her husband was doing the moment that electric currents shoot directly from between her thighs all the way to the top of her head. She tries to understand what it was about this moment: Was the man watching her in a certain way? Was there something else that was unexpected? She thinks it was the moment when he simply saw her, all of her, just standing facing him. That's when she got lost, inundated by a wave of tremendous pleasure.

Maya's husband likes older women. He's somewhat embarrassed to tell her, but often it's very old women that he's attracted to. Why, she asks him. He doesn't know. He thinks that just like pedophiles want to control little girls he wants an old woman to look after him, perhaps to control him. For the most part Maya does control him in daily life, something they both agree on. Now in bed he looks at her the way she likes but imagines her as an old woman. He knows that this is one of those things he can't tell her. She heard it once and didn't like it. He won't ruin the moment and he'll keep his fantasies to himself. But afterwards he thinks that Maya actually knows. And so they sleep together, she imagining that someone is peeping at her while he imagines that she is an old woman. What's wrong with that?

In their everyday life, Maya's husband understands how much she needs attention, not only to be seen naked as in her orgasm fantasy but to feel that she is being seen. He doesn't get worked up about her feminist theories either. He knows that as soon as he "sees" her, the theories will dissipate even though he thinks they are correct. She tries to be a good old woman, knowing that he is dependent on her and waits to hear what she says, and she tries not to take advantage of this. After all, she already cheated on him once, in her imagination, but now she understands how much he needs her.

16. FUCKING ME IN EVERY HOLE

A bigail came for therapy because she is thirty-five and doesn't have a steady boyfriend. She wants a man who knows what to do with women. This phrase bothers her female therapist who would not want a man who "knows what to do," because she is not a machine that needs to be operated correctly. Abigail then tells her how she sleeps with men on their first date. "Why?" the therapist asks. "To check if it's a good fit," Abigail replies, surprised by the question. "Sex is important."

The therapist already has a hypothesis about Abigail's orgasm fantasy, one that often appears in relations with the opposite sex. Abigail "beautifully" explains an experience of degradation.

Abigail says that when she masturbates, she imagines she "is being fucked in every hole." She envisions being entered from the front, from behind, and in the mouth as well. "It's not rape," she explains. "I am cooperating." "But what do you feel?" the therapist probes. Abigail thinks it over and admits that she feels humiliation – precisely then she comes. She has another fantasy in which someone comes on to her on the bus and then undresses her. She tries to refuse as the other passengers are looking but not intervening. The man lays her down on the floor and the moment he penetrates her she surrenders to her body and climaxes.

What happened during the critical period in which Abigail's orgasm fantasy developed? Perhaps Abigail's fantasy that she is "being fucked in every hole" is really the sense of humiliation she felt as a baby as several people, including her mother and other family members, simultaneously gathered around her, and possibly a deep sense that others are using her even though she is enjoying being the center of attention. One can imagine this type of ridicule that the baby Abigail internalized, until this became her default way of relating to the world. We always need to bear in mind that what the baby experiences in all its fragility will generally not be seen from the outside by others in the family. As for sex on the bus in front of an audience, perhaps, for example, Abigail's mother humiliated her during the critical period of the "imprinting of the fantasy" in the presence of other family members. Her mother may have scolded her, laughed at her, and encouraged others to join in. The two fantasies seem to be very similar.

In response to the therapist's question about her dreams, Abigail recounts a recurrent childhood dream in which she is alone in the sea and her mother who was on the beach has disappeared. The beach suddenly disappears as well, the sun sets and she is swimming all alone in the world. In another dream that recurs in different variations, she is driving in a car with her mother. She accelerates, the needle reaches 150 kilometers-per-hour and for some reason she continues pressing the gas pedal. She then awakens with a start, covered in a cold sweat. Abigail's therapist thinks that long stories about the early relations between Abigail and her mother cannot depict as well as dreams how Abigail really feels about her mother, namely, that she can neither live with her nor without her.

Abigail is the CEO of a successful high-tech company. She admits that she is tough with employees and cuts through things like a knife. She has also heard that people say she is mean. But when a friend refuses to give Abigail a bite of her popsicle, she is hurt and could even end the relationship over it. She has the same reaction if a friend arrives late for a meeting. "Where does this sensitivity come from?" she asks her therapist. "Where does this vulnerability come from?" she corrects herself. The therapist understands that in Abigail's conscious third level of thinking there are strengths, capabilities, and toughness. But where does the vulnerability really come from? From the first level? The second? Or maybe from these two levels of thinking together?

Abigail was raised by her mother; her father was a sickly type who was barely involved. She remembers her mother encouraging her in school, being pleased with her outstanding grades, but also sometimes saying unpleasant things to her. "She was a school principal. The students were afraid of her and said she was tough but I thought she was warm." "What sort of unpleasant things did she say to you?" the therapist asks. "For example, that I have bad breath and therefore guys won't come near me. Once I went out with a guy a few years younger than me and my mother asked me if I was screwing children." "Why?" the therapist asks, shocked. "Why?" Abigail doesn't know; she thinks it was meant to be a joke. "Were you offended?" Abigail thinks for a moment and remembers that she was indeed offended.

In the conscious third level of thinking Abigail identifies with her mother's aggression as well as her encouragement, and she runs the company firmly and successfully. Something good did come out of all this after all. Abigail's first and second levels of thinking, however, tell a different story, namely how her mother's aggression made her so vulnerable.

Many successful people had orgasm fantasies that might seem unusual (Anna Freud had an orgasm fantasy in which she is being beaten; Heinz Kohut had an orgasm fantasy in which he was raped by a stronger woman; at the precise moment that he was doing his utmost to fulfill her wishes he would reach climax).

Abigail's therapist tries to get close to her and offer her warmth. It is clear to her that this is what Abigail most needs, a warm mother, a different experience from her orgasm fantasy and her nighttime dreams, while retaining awareness of them. This new experience could enable her to form a non-humiliating relationship with a man. At the door, Abigail asks her for a hug. The therapist is hesitant. In their next session it transpires that Abigail felt very hurt. The therapist tries to apologize, to explain that it's not accepted. Abigail quits therapy. Her wound was too deep to accept such explanations.

Toward the end of her brief therapy, Abigail revealed another orgasm fantasy in which a female physical fitness trainer is holding her tightly and other women are inserting fingers and other objects into her vagina and playing with her clitoris. The trainer orders her to climax. Again, the moment of greatest humiliation is the moment of pleasure. This time as well the therapist was not surprised, and felt that she was practically waiting to hear this kind of fantasy. The development of the lesbian fantasy can be attributed to Abigail's mother having been distant, cold and tough during the critical period in which the fantasy was shaped. This is how homosexual relationships develop, a retreat from the third level of thinking to the second and sexual level when something is lacking in the baby girl's relationship with the mother figure or the baby boy's relationship with the father figure. In this situation, a relationship that is meant to express warmth and closeness leading to identification, is transformed into a sexual relationship. Many cases of homosexuality can apparently be explained in this way. Moreover, again we see that the type of relationship in the orgasm fantasy (a humiliating one in this case) does not change whether or not it is directed to a man or a woman. This is the repressed bisexual nature we all share.

Improving sex and relationships

Abigail met a man and following her therapist's advice did not go to bed with him the first night. This was not easy for her. He is a sensitive, gentle guy who actually liked her power and strength. Soon he will also discover her orgasm fantasy. This usually comes later and then things start becoming interesting...

In bed he suggests that Abigail choose her favorite fantasy. She wants to be fucked at work, on her desk, the CEO's desk, in front of all the employees. She wants to give them all something because she thinks the way she treated them was humiliating and that they deserve compensation. The boyfriend tells her that he is one of the employees, how they are having sex on top of the desk in front of everyone, how much he is enjoying it, and how much he appreciates what she is giving him. Suddenly she starts coming and he starts laughing. Abigail thinks that it's actually the laughter that helps her find the middle path with the employees, to be neither tough nor too soft. She is now able to recognize both extremes and understands why she flees into being tough with her staff so as not to surrender and give them everything. In bed with the boyfriend, she also comes to understand why she loves her mother: "Maybe we're similar," she tells him, "she too was tough with me so as not to break down and totally give in to me."

The boyfriend thinks that the way he handles Abigail is a lot more successful than any psychological intervention.

He touches on the real things and doesn't just engage in intellectual bullshit. Abigail seems to agree.

Abigail's boyfriend comes when he simultaneously suckles and penetrates her. He is ashamed to tell Abigail what is going through his mind but with a bit of urging he relents and tells her that when he is sucking and penetrating he feels he is getting everything he wants from a woman – from below and above. He is dazzled in both directions. He is sure that suckling babies obtain satisfaction from it, and that Freud's theory is correct. When she strokes his head and lets him come below and above, he wants her to hold him tight as he comes. His mother never held him this way, he suddenly reveals to her. Something in Abigail relaxes even more, and all at once he is her baby and not her partner; she lets him penetrate in the best way possible, relaxes and gives him her all. For a moment she really is a mother.

In their next quarrel he won't understand how he let such a crazy woman be his mother, and she won't understand how she let such a baby that she wouldn't even hire teach her something important about her life. She will mock him for always feeling small and weak and needing to be hugged as in his orgasm fantasy. He will imitate her coming while everyone fucks her. Then they will again make up and go to bed. He tells her how he fucks her in front of everyone, while in his imagination he is the baby receiving everything from his mother, both penetration and suckling. She tells him how wonderful it is that he is suckling while she imagines she is being fucked in every hole. Over and over they learn to recognize the fantasies that direct the reality of their lives.

17. THREESOME

3 3 -year-old Arya, a tall, beautiful blonde in high heels, as her male therapist describes her, enters the clinic. She doesn't walk in confidently. First she peeks to see if the therapist is there even though this is her scheduled time. She takes a seat in the armchair, provocatively clad in an evening dress with a very high slit on the side and a plunging neckline that shows off her ample cleavage. Her smile is seductive.

She came for therapy because she wants to break up with her 22-year-old boyfriend and hasn't been able to do so. Every time the breakup is imminent, she develops a strange and annoying rash all over her body. Thorough medical examinations, she adds with a little laugh, failed to turn up any pathological cause. It's all in her head. On her conscious third level of thinking, Arya is clearly anxious. Does her provocative attire reflect aggression? This, at least, is what her therapist, who finds himself shrinking in his armchair at her appearance, senses. So apparently there is also aggression in her conscious third level of thinking.

In this case, we lack significant information about Arya's childhood. She also doesn't remember her dreams. But her boyfriend says that she sometimes yells in the middle of the night, "Let me go! Let me go!" accompanied by beating the pillow. Indeed, Arya seems to feel deep inside that this man is not for her but she is incapable of taking the necessary step and breaking up with him, a step that is related to her conscious third level of thinking in which she is anxious. However, the testimony from her unconscious first level of thinking, the dream level, could help Arya connect to her repressed desire to break up. Without this testimony, she would probably be even more confused.

The therapist asks her about her orgasm fantasy. The provocative Arya is embarrassed, she doesn't hasten to answer. She ponders the question and smiles awkwardly. The therapist explains to her the importance of the fantasy in understanding her relations with the world. She accepts the explanation and is prepared to respond. When she imagines her boyfriend with another woman, especially when she sees his face contorted with pleasure, and hears the sounds he makes, she immediately climaxes. Sometimes she is the one who brings him the other women and readies them for him: She undresses them, bathes them and lays them down on the bed. Then when he sleeps with them she is already totally "hot" and climaxes immediately. "His pleasure drives me wild," she explains. "I don't know why but I can't resist it." She admits though that she is hesitant to talk about this because it humiliates her and pains her very much that in her imagination he sleeps with other women and not with her. The therapist suggests that she feels small and undeserving. The big people are having sex and she is watching them. This resonates with her. She recalls that her parents were often busy with each other and not paying attention to her.

She then describes her boyfriend's complementary orgasm fantasy. He wants to sleep with a woman while she, his girlfriend, is watching them have fun. "He can come just from my hurt and jealous expression. It feels kind of sadistic," she says, "he's also that way with other people, seemingly unintentionally. Maybe that's why I'm so jealous. Maybe because I'm afraid that I'll fulfill my sexual fantasies with him." Indeed this is how the conscious third level of thinking is often shaped in relation to the second level of the orgasm fantasy, in this case, in order to prevent its fulfillment.

She remembers an incident from the start of their relationship in which her boyfriend begged her to let him sleep with her best friend. "At that point we weren't really boyfriend and girlfriend yet, which is maybe why I wasn't so jealous." She remains silent, with a hint of a smile. The therapist finds it difficult to contain his curiosity. "And what happened?" he asks. "No, nothing happened, but it scares me so much that I'm capable of agreeing just so I can see his face."

"All men are the same," Arya continues. "They only want sex." She knows this and she drives them wild. She can get anyone she wants into bed with her. The therapist interrupts to ask if she thinks she could also get him into bed. Arya stops in the middle: "Well I'm not sure about that," she wavers and smiles. The therapist thinks that Arya is now speaking from her conscious third level of thinking in which she is aggressive. He suggests to her that she may be compensating for a deep feeling of humiliation in the second level of her orgasm fantasy. He reminds her that in her orgasm fantasy she is watching from the side and suddenly at the conscious third level of thinking she is bedding anybody she wants.

Arya seems to ignore her therapist's comment and continues explaining with a triumphant expression why all men are the same. Recently she was detained for questioning because she was caught with drugs. She behaved seductively toward the detective at the police station and that night she slept with him at his home and reached orgasms with him of a power that simply terrified her – a total loss of control. The therapist, reluctantly, actually believes her. She seems capable of doing such things, and also of reaching such sexual heights – perhaps because of her hysterical side.

Arya feels sure that her therapist wants her to find some uninspiring fellow but she knows that this is not for her. She recently tried to form a relationship with a nerdy guy who studies computer science at the university. He took the bus to pick her up, didn't pay for her and, worst of all, didn't know how to have sex. "An egalitarian relationship is not for you," the therapist comments sarcastically. "You want a policeman."

Arya starts talking about her teenage years and how she boldly experimented with sexual adventures and drugs. At seventeen, she was raped. She thinks that one of her friends put something in her drink to make her fall asleep and then everyone raped her. She doesn't describe this with any hint of trauma, but rather calmly and naturally. When the therapist inquires how she felt about the incident, she immediately says that it didn't have much of an impact on her. Her calm affect with no signs of repression or distress, leads the therapist to believe her yet again. The above raises the question about the connection between a rape victim's orgasm fantasy and her trauma in the wake of the rape. Arya's awareness of her sexuality and especially of her orgasm fantasy could mitigate the trauma of the rape (See the discussion of rape in the afterword).

Arya quit therapy after a few halting and non-consecutive sessions. She assured the therapist that she would return when she was a little calmer and more settled. A valuable insight nonetheless...

Improving sex and relationships

Arya could become attracted to her "nerd." She needs to imagine that he is having sex with her girlfriend and that she is watching them. She will imagine his face contorting with pleasure, the out-of-control sounds that he makes... Then her jealousy will rise and she will turn him into a man in her imagination. Her awareness of her orgasm fantasy will also help her to develop control of it in her daily life rather than being controlled by it. For this, she needs a little more help through therapy. Then she won't need in her imagination to bed everyone so as not to be humiliated by them, and her sexual provocations will decrease somewhat. At the same time, her jealousy of her partner will also abate because the difference between fantasy and reality will be clearer. The truth is that both men and women who are having trouble feeling attracted to their partner whom they respect and with whom they wish to spend their lives may use this technique and find it helpful (See the afterword).

Arya may discover that her nerd is actually the first guy with whom she can not only share details of her orgasm fantasy but can also play with fantasies more than with all of her macho boyfriends. "He fills me with confidence," she will say. "With him, I don't feel threatened and I can envision all my 'perverted' fantasies. I was always scared to tell other guys about my orgasm fantasy lest they exploit it, cheat on me and tell me that it's what I really wanted." Arya will learn – what we all need to know – that in order to freely play with fantasies, she has to feel secure. Hopefully, this feeling is something her nerdy boyfriend can provide her in generous supply.

Arya's boyfriend is a rather weird guy, successful in high-tech, but withdrawn and self-involved. Arya complains that she is the one who has to call him to set up a date. Sometimes she has the feeling that if she didn't do this, they wouldn't have a relationship. He replies that she just doesn't give him a chance to call, but always calls him first. However, when he told Arya his orgasm fantasy, it was easier for her to accept his behavior by understanding that this is who he really is. In his fantasy he is lying on his back and a girl is going down on him. This way, he tells Arya, he feels like a king. His job is not to make an effort and therefore he has a special servant girl who does the work. Now it is easier for Arya to call him and to do the work, while he, her nerd, never forgets to remind her each time how great she is and how she deserves to have everything.

18. PARADISE

Victoria sits facing her female therapist who hardly manages to say anything. Is this because Victoria doesn't let her get a word in, or maybe because the therapist senses how vulnerable she is. Whatever the therapist says, Victoria immediately takes issue, even if only in her body language. Something isn't right for her in the room, whether the armchair and the cushions or the therapist herself. Maybe she just wants the therapist to be quiet, which she is prepared to do, but for how long! It would seem that Victoria needs her therapist to be totally empathic towards her, endlessly sensitive, or perhaps invisible and unfeeling in order not to hurt her. Simply breathing and barely saying anything triggers a struggle.

Victoria spends much of her time surfing dating websites. She wants a man. Maybe this is why she chose a female therapist who would understand the urgency of her search. However, she also leaves these websites feeling very hurt. She dreamed that a gentle guy was caressing her and then went to caress other girls. She understands that this is the feeling she gets from the dating websites, namely that she is not alone there. In another dream she is being attacked by crocodiles with protruding tongues, which she understands to be how she experiences all the men on the dating websites who are only looking for sex and not a real relationship. There was also a dream in which she is peeing in the street and everyone sees her. She says this is how she feels with her profile on the dating sites.

Victoria is clearly anxious both during the day and at night. In the clinic in her conscious third level of thinking it is very striking, but is also apparent in her unconscious first level of thinking, her dreams. The therapist realizes that she has to be as empathic as possible. Still, Victoria's orgasm fantasy surprises her.

"There is no clear picture there, more like pleasant floating sensations. Maybe it's paradise," Victoria says. When she sees this floating pinkness, she climaxes. The therapist presses a little. Maybe there's something arousing in this paradise that she hasn't told her about? "No, there really isn't. Streams? Trees?" Victoria asks herself and the answer is negative. "It's just this euphoric feeling that envelops me. The color pink expresses it best. Then, when I'm in the midst of this sensation, I climax."

In her first year of life her father was more involved in raising her than her mother. He was a very anxious man, distant and ineffectual, and he conveyed his anxieties to her. The therapist can see in Victoria's dreams that only the anxiety is present without any helpful characters. With other patients who have anxious but warm and affectionate parents, one can see threats and dangers in their dreams alongside good and helpful characters, which is not the case in Victoria's dreams. Thus the dream exemplifies how one can identify with his or her parents and their personality characteristics along with the internalization of the parents' attitude toward the baby.

Around her second year of life, it was Victoria's mother who took care of her. She was a simple but very warm woman who created for her an experience of paradise in which the two of them were together and anything was possible. Afterwards Victoria grew up, her needs increased, and her parents turned out to be increasingly helpless in the larger world. The therapist thinks she understands: In Victoria's first year of life she sensed her father's constant anxiety and everything went without words into her unconscious first level of dreams. In the second year of life, her mother functioned well, the child began to walk and talk, to construct slightly longer sentences and started to learn about cleanliness. This is the time that a child discovers and swallows the world with wide-open eyes, and Victoria's mother joined her in this magical world. Then, when the third conscious level of thinking develops and a higher level of functioning is necessary, again anxieties emerge.

So what then happens to Victoria in the clinic when she hungers for paradise with her therapist who is an "incompetent" person who cannot give her the perfection she has been seeking ever since those rosy days with her mother? She becomes dissatisfied, critical and angry. Ultimately she will also quit therapy. But this is exactly what happens to her with men as well. Her therapist has already told her many times to be more forgiving and more flexible with men, and that no one is perfect – including her. Intellectually Victoria agrees. She is an intelligent woman but lacks emotional intelligence. And so she haughtily rejects all the guys on the dating sites.

The therapist tries again by explaining to her that she has been trying her whole life to recreate her lost paradise manifested in her orgasm fantasy, and when she fails she becomes in her conscious third level of thinking anxious or angry. Such a fantasy of paradise is not necessarily good, and the question remains what Victoria does when it doesn't come true.

Later she dreamed that someone was giving her something to eat that she didn't like, and how she was sleeping with someone whose penis was too big. This world, she is beginning to see, is not the right fit for her. Her therapist, who tries so hard to help her, isn't right for her either.

Victoria quits therapy claiming that her therapist doesn't understand her well enough. Victoria has previously left seven other therapists and is still searching for her private paradise but pushing everyone out of it.

Improving sex and relationships

Later, Victoria met a man some years older than her. The father she never had, she says without hesitation. And she, apparently, is the daughter he never had. He tries to create a paradise for her and often even succeeds. Yes, such miracles happen. Where the therapist failed, the boyfriend succeeded. He does not interpret her behavior or try to get her to understand it. He is simply with her and loving, perhaps as her mother was with her way back in her early childhood. When they sleep together, Victoria returns to her personal paradise, to her color pink. The boyfriend waits for her to climax, "first her and then me," he says. Victoria does indeed need his full attention. In paradise, things are done in a relaxed way and the boyfriend enters her gently, gazing into her eyes to see if she is still there. And then the unbelievable happens – Victoria suddenly sees fireworks in different colors in her paradise. She knows that this is not part of paradise, because she knows the story. Now the two of them are laughing. And what about the boyfriend? "Ladies first," he always says to her, but now it's his turn.

Victoria thinks that her boyfriend's generosity comes from his conscious third level of thinking. He is like this with everyone. She knows how important it is for him to be a good person and to be perceived as such. But his orgasm fantasy surprised Victoria as well. He does not want to penetrate her, but only to masturbate while Victoria watches. As she watches closely and he continues to masturbate and sees that she is watching, he suddenly erupts with boundless pleasure. He wonders why that look of hers drives him so wild.

When Victoria's boyfriend is with his friends he likes to talk and have others listen. "But with me," Victoria says, "he is just the opposite. He lets me talk and listens with undivided attention." With his friends, Victoria's boyfriend recreates his orgasm fantasy in which he is at the center and everyone is looking at him, but when he is with Victoria he recreates his conscious third level of thinking in which it is important to him to be generous.

Victoria's boyfriend knows that when she is not in her paradise she may be anxious, and has learned to accept her anxiety. He also knows that he can calm her by talking to her and returning her to paradise, which fills him with importance and makes their relationship especially warm and loving. Victoria thinks that in these moments he is like the good parent she didn't have. For her part, she has learned how much her boyfriend sometimes needs her and others to see him and pay attention to him. But she still doesn't really understand what his parents did to him to bring about such an orgasm fantasy.

19. PINNING HER DOWN BY THE ARMS AND THEN...

This is how Joseph dominates his girlfriend. He pins her arms down tightly so she can't move. It's very important that she not be able to move. Then he performs cunnilingus on her very slowly and in complete control. Not too fast and not too slow. He feels the heartbeats of her moaning body getting stronger together with the tempo of his work. "This control is very precise," he explains with a smile to his female therapist. "The moment of climax is approaching. I remain cool and composed. Then, when she suddenly comes, I am the one who made it happen. All with calculation and control. In this way she is in my hands."

To the therapist's regret, Joseph did not tell her his orgasm fantasy until the end of his lengthy therapy. She knew Joseph very well but the orgasm fantasy gave the "seal of approval" to what had taken her so much time and effort to understand.

Joseph came to therapy because things weren't going well for him. He had changed jobs and professions, and felt inferior to those around him. He is the eldest of four brothers all of whom were more successful than him (engineers and doctors), while he barely finished high school. Sitting around the table at festive gatherings he would usually be silent, letting the smarter ones discuss the state of the nation and other serious matters. For a long time he acted this way from his conscious third level of thinking in which he was particularly anxious. Later, as his therapy progressed he didn't let the others speak at all, this time from the second level of his orgasm fantasy. He would show them that his life's wisdom was no less important than all their degrees. Joseph was actually correct; he really was far from stupid. Of course he was a nationalist Republican and his brothers were intellectual Democrats, and Joseph wasn't sure if he was fighting for the rightness of his positions or just to convey to them: "I'm not as inferior as you think." In truth, Joseph was allowing himself to respond from a different place inside himself. Rather than respond from the conscious third level of his anxious thinking, he began to respond out of his aggressive orgasm fantasy.

To his therapist's disappointment, Joseph did not bring any dreams into the therapy. Some patients try to protect themselves in this way, usually unconsciously. He insisted that he simply doesn't remember his dreams. In the absence of dreams, the therapist had to rely on Joseph's childhood memories: how for years he would cry over every little thing and how his father would immediately run to soothe and comfort him; and how his father would constantly call him home when he was playing outside with friends and how the other kids would tease him about it. He also remembers how once at dinner he told his family about the cuckoo that lays its eggs in the nests of other birds so they will hatch the eggs for them. What he really wanted was to display his knowledge, but he'll never forget the smiles and kicks under the table that followed.

Joseph is filled with anxiety on both the unconscious first level of thinking and the conscious third level of thinking, which were not difficult to observe when he entered the clinic or said goodbye to the therapist on his way out. With a certain hesitation in his body language and speech, he exuded indecision. He never simply says what he wants, and when he does, always hesitates before coming out with it.

He felt that his girlfriend, who was maybe a decade older than him, was far more successful than him, and he was terribly embarrassed that she earned more than he did. In Joseph's conscious third level of thinking, he felt like a cuckoo that knows whom to exploit to do the work for it. He naturally accepted that he should be the one to buy the food, clean the house and maybe also have a nice hot dinner ready when his girlfriend comes home from work. But he could never get over the feeling of humiliation. No, he thinks, he won't let anybody control him. Joseph thus lives with his girlfriend in two contradictory emotional worlds: In his conscious third level of thinking he admires his girlfriend and believes that she is more successful than him, and in his orgasm fantasy he wants to control her or at least for her not to control him.

When Joseph's girlfriend asks him for something, he immediately says "no." Why? Because when he says no he is in control. Now she must wait for him to say "yes." He is never in the mood for sex, which for her, of course, is very insulting. She cries and thinks that maybe he doesn't find her attractive. Suddenly, in the middle of the conversation, he stops his therapist and says to her, "Don't say anything!" as if he is now pinning down his therapist by the arms in his orgasm fantasy, "I'll tell you what you were about to say." As he is usually correct. He is anxious and dependent but certainly not stupid. In reality Joseph was trying to control his therapy and his therapist. If she can't surprise him, then he is in control.

For years the therapist tried to be empathic to Joseph, as she had been taught. To be empathic to his anxieties, his dependency and his weakness in both the unconscious first level of thinking and the conscious third level of thinking. It couldn't be said that there was no progress. Therapists are programmed to be empathic. But Joseph also needed someone who could connect to his aggression, to his orgasm fantasy.

Joseph confessed his little manipulations to the therapist: how he tells his girlfriend to do things that he knows she will do anyway, just to have the feeling that she is doing what he says. When she approaches him, he retreats, thus determining the correct distance. This is how Joseph's orgasm fantasy works – automatically. One wonders how such a fantasy of control developed in the critical period of imprinting in Joseph's relationship with his parents, and how he learned to control them – possibly in order to temper his anxieties and dependency from the unconscious first level of thinking. In this way an island of control in the form of his orgasm fantasy was created in the midst of a sea of anxiety from his first and third levels of thinking.

After a few years into the therapy, the therapist mustered the courage to ask: "Why don't you prepare a nice dinner for yourself and your girlfriend when she comes home tired from work, the kind of romantic dinner with wine and candles that she likes". Joseph doesn't know why not. He is honest enough to say that he will think about it, that it's not easy for him, that she has to accept him as he is, and so on. He did once make an effort, prepared a special dinner for them, and they even slept together afterwards. But this doesn't happen very often. In this particular case, immediately afterward he had the need to tell her that he was traveling abroad with a friend even though they didn't have the money for it, just to feel that he was the one deciding things.

It took years for the therapist to say straightforwardly to Joseph: "You simply want to control your girlfriend, and not only her." For years, this sentence had been softened with phrases like "how hard it is for you" and "how anxious you are," etc. But what about the encounter with reality that the orgasm fantasy expresses so well? Joseph is anxious. This is easy to see in his conscious third level of thinking, but what does he do in the second level of his orgasm fantasy? Orgasm Fantasy Theory enables us, on the one hand, to be empathic, in this case in Joseph's unconscious first level of thinking and the third level of thinking in which his anxieties are conscious, but, on the other hand the theory demands, without blinking, to relate to his aggression in the second level of his orgasm fantasy.

Improving sex and relationships

When Joseph performs his cunnilingus on his girlfriend, he doesn't know what is going through her mind. It's probably not what Joseph thinks, if he thinks about it at all. It's true that she is experiencing orgasms one after the other and he doesn't stop until she begs him to. This pleading makes him feel good too. Then, in order to maintain control, he suggests that she climax just once more, and she usually agrees. It's like when children are told to stop banging on something and they need to bang just one more time. But in those precious moments that he goes down on her, she imagines that men are saying she is "the best fuck in the world" and that they lose control when they see her. She pictures them standing in line to lick her, each one getting only a few seconds. Indeed, in observing Joseph's girlfriend, it is almost possible to identify this orgasm fantasy: She is a very sexy woman who knows how to dress and is aware that men are gazing at her. There is also something impulsive and hysterical about her that perhaps makes it possible to predict this fantasy. However, as we have said, in her conscious third level of thinking she is an ambitious, talented and very organized person and it's no wonder that she is so successful at her job.

Only recently did she reveal her orgasm fantasy to Joseph. He now makes a special effort, whispers in her ear that she is the best fuck in the world, that he is dying to fuck her and can't hold back. She goes crazy with pleasure. Often he lets his imagination run wild and describes to her how irresistible men find her, which also sends her into a frenzy. Joseph begins to understand how imperative it is for his girlfriend to feel important, to be at the center of everything, and to be admired by others – not only regarding sex. He also comes to realize how much anguish he causes her when he tries to place himself in the center instead of her. Knowing what makes her feel good makes it easier for him to forgo his fantasy of control. Recently, for example, when she approaches him he doesn't move away but rather gazes at her with open pleasure. This is exactly what makes her happy, she says, this admiring gaze. She, meanwhile, recognizes Joseph's feelings of inferiority from his conscious third level of thinking and frequently points out the smart things he says and how original, beautiful and interesting his ideas are. Now when he is trying to control her, which still happens fairly often despite his awareness, she is less offended. Her familiarity with Joseph's orgasm fantasy helps her to better understand and accept him.

As they raise a toast while enjoying the dinner that Joseph prepared for them, they look each other in the eye and say with a little laugh: "Cheers to the one who wants to be in control, and cheers to the one who wants to be admired." And they are so happy because they understand that there is no contradiction between any fantasies as long as instead of hiding them, people are prepared to play with them.

20. THE THERAPIST HAS AN ORGASM FANTASY TOO

Lisa enters the clinic with packages. It's not clear where she's coming from or where she's going. Sagging and bent over, her curly hair looks sticky and neglected. Maybe not quite that severe, but that's the general impression she conveys. She sits down on the couch, sighs, and then lies down. She has no energy to speak; she's panting and her chest is heaving. Depression? Certainly possible. Soon she will turn fifty, she wants a partner, a boyfriend for life, maybe to adopt some kids and build the family she has never had. But, wait a minute; she doesn't even have a job.

She wants the male therapist to speak, to ask questions. In her home, no one asked her anything, so now she wants him to ask. The story of her childhood? A few dreams will suffice. In one, she is walking alone in the desert on the way back to her childhood home. Her mouth is filled with dust, her breathing is labored, she is weary and thirsty but keeps walking. Finally she arrives and meets her father. He asks her why she came and she doesn't know how to answer. Then her mother tells her that if she comes without a boyfriend she can go away. Afterwards, they spoke on the phone, this time for real; as usual her parents did all the talking and she just listened. She put down the receiver and let them speak. She came back five minutes later and they hadn't even noticed her absence. This, too, is a kind of relationship.

In another dream her father pulls down his pants and pees in the living room. Why? There's something crude and sexual about him, she says. He tosses his "dirt" everywhere. But at least he listens a little. Her mother doesn't listen at all. Afterwards, walking in the street at night, she ran into a group of friends from high school who didn't stop taunting her. "In other dreams they just ignore me," she explains to the therapist. What an inner world, the therapist thinks. Who needs facts?!

In her conscious third level of thinking, her daydreams, Lisa is aware that she is constantly angry. She wants to curse and hit everyone, she tells her therapist. She imagines what they are saying to her and how she replies. "At least you have strength," the therapist tells her, "you fight and don't give in." She then says she has fantasies of how she tortures people so they should feel what she feels, hinting at sexual abuse, although it will take her a while to reveal what exactly she does to them. It later transpires that she pictures herself castrating men with a knife, one after the other, any of them who ever insulted her, so that they should know how it feels and above all so they should regret what they did to her. The therapist wishes to hear details (what exactly she did to these men) in order to understand the depth of her experience of cruelty, but cannot bring himself to ask and says nothing.

Lisa is always changing partners. Even though she is ostensibly searching for a relationship she doesn't know how to create a connection. "How is a connection made?" she asks. She says that maybe it's hard for her to build trust, which is how a relationship is formed. She is always on the receiving end; everyone is always being cruel to her. And she is as helpless and miserable as can be. This is another current in her conscious third level of thinking in addition to the anger – a current of wretchedness.

The therapist feels sexually aroused. He, too, has an orgasm fantasy of which he is aware. But what is it about Lisa that arouses him in this way? Maybe her wretchedness plays into his aggression? Maybe her helplessness invites exploitation?

Lisa says that at least when it comes to the sexual side of things, she can be proud. She has no problem achieving orgasm and she gets a lot of pleasure from sex. In her orgasm fantasy she sees a large penis unrelentingly penetrating her vagina. She feels the pain in her womb, but doesn't give in to the pain. She spreads her legs wider and continues to masturbate, wanting it to hurt. Sometimes it's not pain but rather a good feeling of something that fills up all the inner space between her legs. It feels to her as if she is containing something. "A woman is containment," she tells her therapist, "which is why women can contain more than men". Then, amid all this ongoing pain or feeling of physical and emotional containment, she suddenly starts to feel the orgasm slowly crawling up her thighs, in her vagina and in her head with unbearable intensity. "Pain and pleasure are the same thing," she explains to her therapist. She read somewhere that they both come from the same place in the brain which doesn't surprise her.

In the first two levels of thinking, the first unconscious level, her dreams, and the second level of the orgasm fantasy, Lisa feels like a victim, passive and vulnerable. It's true she enjoys sex, but the pleasure has a masochistic aspect to it. But what about her real life? The therapist must first help her to understand her victim-like position in her orgasm fantasy and afterwards to understand her anger and wretchedness in her conscious third level of thinking. In bed, she excels and certainly doesn't need his help.

No, the therapist doesn't have the courage to tell her what she arouses in him, although he is aware that it's something that comes from her and that other female patients don't produce similar feelings in him. But it is important for Lisa to know what feelings she arouses in others because one can assume that she did not invent this for her therapist's sake. But can he really tell her that he is getting an erection during their therapy sessions?

There are many ways of talking to her about the wretchedness she conveys to the world. But there is nothing stronger and more alive than what is happening here and now, which is what he was taught in the long years of training to become a certified psychologist. Another therapist might not turn her into a sexual object. Then too he could be accused of sexually exploiting his female patients; in the current #MeToo era, anything is possible. He has yet to hear of a therapist who tells his female patient about the erection she induces in him and to explore the reason with her.

Recently Lisa has started also to criticize the therapist. In her imagination, he too has become someone who hurts her. She says he is not nice to her, doesn't find time for her and doesn't understand her exactly as she wants him to.

The room is empty, the words evaporate, the interval between the words grows, silence prevails. Twilight. If he would have fucked her, he would have really brought her to life. Of that he is certain. She wants to be filled up, after all. This is what arouses her and fills her with life. He has already heard that she knows how to enjoy sex, and that many men enjoy having sex with her. But this is just sex, not life. He would like her to see how she becomes a victim in her orgasm fantasy, and how furious she is in her conscious thinking.

He won't tell her what she arouses in him, for he is simply a coward. But thanks to his awareness of these feelings, he can help her recognize what she arouses in others.

Improving sex and relationships

Lisa has already had many different kinds of boyfriend, including a sex maniac who wanted to sleep with her ten times a day until she couldn't take it anymore, and an impotent guy who had no interest in sex and only wanted them to live together like siblings. Recently she met someone whose orgasm fantasy is that of understanding a girl, literally. He is a doctor, listens intently to his patients, is extremely empathic, understands their pain, and then suddenly in the midst of this listening as he is all wrapped up in his female patient, he suddenly feels a warm and pleasant discharge in his underwear. This is a little frightening, it's also a little unpleasant, but he goes on talking with the patient as if nothing has happened. Sometimes the spreading stain on his pants is visible but he counts on the patient not noticing. Yes, Lisa's boyfriend reaches orgasm when he understands a girl. What girl wouldn't want someone like that? But, as with every orgasm fantasy, it's not entirely good.

Lisa's boyfriend had a depressive mother who simply wanted to die. When he was very young he tried to understand her and breathe life into her with this understanding. This is how a baby perceives his mother and adapts himself to her needs. With his infantile instincts, Lisa's boyfriend felt that if he would understand his mother she wouldn't be so alone and he too wouldn't end up alone. This is how his orgasm of understanding came into being. When he meets people he spontaneously always tries to please them. He is totally attentive to them, reaffirms what they say, and essentially negates himself, which is how his orgasm of understanding manifests itself in everyday life. He also has a recurrent daydream that unfortunately reinforces his orgasm fantasy. In the daydream he is always number two, never number one. He is always helping someone superior to himself. In his medical department he is known as the department head's loyal right-hand man. When he was offered a promotion he immediately proposed that it go to another colleague because she is better than him and more suited to the job. On his soccer team, as well, in which he is an outstanding player, he always declines to be the captain. The cost of the angry outbursts of someone who is so understanding of others in his orgasm fantasy, and who chooses to be number two in his conscious third level of thinking, in his daydreams, is something we shall discuss later. Clearly, though, everything has a price, which Lisa is paying.

Now, in bed, he tells her what a huge penis he has, even though the reality is far removed. He penetrates her, she asks him not to move so that she can feel the pain of containment. He is with her, he understands her wish exactly, as no man has ever understood her before. She asks him to move, she wants a little more pain. He moves forward and backward. He tells her that this really hurts her. Suddenly the two of them reach orgasm simultaneously, he from a full understanding of her, and she from the pain of containment that is now climbing up from her womb to her head. She laughs, saying that she doesn't care at all that he has a small penis. He isn't insulted; he understands her now as well.

Having finished they are free to contemplate their lives. He tells her how important it is that she not invite everyone to make her a victim – just as she asked him to hurt her – and then get angry as a result. And if she wants to castrate all the men in her head, she can go right ahead. It's fine with him as long as he is not on the list, because that's where his understanding and his ability to be accepting will end. She tells him how much she wants him to get ahead in his department and to be number one because that's what he deserves, and that he should stop groveling to the whole world, and to her as well. "Then you really will have a big dick," she says, smiling, and he knows that it's an affirmation of love.

21. GENTLE CARESSES

Valentina has an orgasm fantasy in which she sees a group of men and women caressing one another as if in a mass orgy. She thinks she's one of the figures in the orgy, but she's not sure if she's a man or a woman or whether she's caressing a man or a woman. What she does know is that the caresses are very gentle. Again we see in people with bisexual tendencies what we don't see with heterosexuals, namely, a fantasy in which the relations are the same whether directed at women or at men.

When it seems to Valentina that she is a man in her orgasm fantasy, she feels stressed. Her female therapist reassures her that it is only a fantasy. Indeed, there is something masculine about 25-year-old Valentina's body language. She is also aware of this; maybe it's her forceful movements or her confident stride. But Valentina is a blonde, blue-eyed woman with the face of an angel and has never thought about becoming a man. She also has a husband whom she loves.

Moreover, Valentina is a very gentle person who, despite her masculine movements, creates gentle relationships with everyone, including her therapist, as in her orgasm fantasy, which reflects her masculine gentleness to an amazing degree. She likes to tenderly caress her husband as in her orgasm fantasy and he loves the touch of her warm hand. It's not sexual, she explains to her therapist, even though the therapist doesn't entirely believe it, it's more maternal. In fact, Valentina's mother is very warm and affectionate, and so far there is nothing particularly surprising here.

The therapy began with drama because Valentina was unwilling to lie on the couch. She was afraid her therapist would do something to her, especially since she wished to sit behind Valentina's head, so that she would see Valentina, but Valentina wouldn't see her. Valentina finally agreed to lie on the couch on condition that the therapist would sit in the armchair facing her. The therapist agreed. These, of course, were anxieties from the conscious third level of thinking. After several sessions, the therapist told her that the privileges were over and that she would now sit wherever she wanted. Valentina protested and threatened to quit therapy. The therapist simply told her that in her clinic, she's the one who decides. Valentina continued to lie on the couch her fists clenched. The therapist asked if she wanted to hit her. Valentina blurted out with a sigh of relief: "That's brilliant." "What's brilliant?" the therapist asked. "What you did," Valentina replied. "Now I don't need to feel sorry for you, I'm exempt from this punishment. Now it'll be easier for me to be myself, because you allow yourself to be yourself."

We have a paradox here. On the one hand, Valentina displays aggression in her masculine body language and her clenched fists when she is angry, while on the other she is telling us how, in her conscious third level of thinking, she feels sorry for everyone and has trouble expressing anger. In her second level of thinking, her orgasm fantasy, there are only "gentle caresses" and no manifestations of aggression. If in her first level of thinking, her dreams, we also don't find expressions of assertiveness or aggression, we will ask ourselves: Where has the aggression in Valentina's body language disappeared to? Furthermore, we will ask ourselves how we can encourage Valentina to be more assertive, which, as we have seen, is vital to any sense of strength and confidence, when this emotion doesn't exist in any of her three levels of thinking.

The many dreams that Valentina brought to the sessions from the start of therapy provide the best insight into her story. In one dream, she and her mother were in a room that was floating high in the air. Valentina opened the door and was frightened by the abyss she saw below. Despite the danger and the fear, she and her mother didn't exchange a word. It seems that this is how Valentina experienced her life, being in constant danger but unable to communicate with her mother. Why? At home, she says, they never talked, not even in times of distress.

In another dream she was with her family in a forest. People scattered and each time someone else got lost. Valentina ran from one to another, trying to bring them together and keep them safe. Suddenly her father lost consciousness and started having a seizure. Only Valentina saw this. She tried to resuscitate him but without success. These two dreams tell the story of Valentina's relations with her parents and the world in a nutshell: they won't protect her and she can only expect anxiety and loneliness.

It seems that a person may feel only loneliness, gentleness, and victimhood in all three levels of thinking, even though his body language expresses aggression and anger. In this situation, the individual projects his aggression on to the other in such a way that it will not appear in any of his three levels of thinking. How then can Valentina identify these feelings, relate to them and express them when necessary? Moreover, we know that if Valentina were to become aware of her anger and direct her aggression outward, her anxieties (which we have seen in her first and third levels of thinking) would be moderated. We have seen this before and we also understand that anxiety is really repressed aggression that is self-directed.

On the couch her voice breaks, and she finds it hard to talk. Everyone in the world is wretched and so is she. She wants children but her husband isn't yet ready. How long will she have to wait? But she also knows that in order to be a good mother she first has to truly be herself, which is precisely what is difficult for her. The therapist asks her to keep an anger diary. She explains to her that when she is crying in her conscious third level of thinking, she is actually angry. The same goes for when she is anxious. She further explains that they aren't seeing anger in any of her three levels of thinking. She just doesn't know how to be angry, whether during the day or at night, or even in her orgasm fantasy. This is the missing emotion or the "absent fantasy" in her world.

Valentina is a doctor and a good student. She keeps the anger diary in which she records in detail every overt or suppressed anger that she notices. Before long, a huge amount of anger has surfaced that she previously had never let herself feel. This is what happens when a person who is never angry, even in dreams, suddenly discovers it. The longer she kept the anger diary, the more her dreams changed. More dreams about loneliness began to appear and fewer dreams about anxiety. In one dream she was walking with girlfriends and went to buy an ice cream, but when she returned the friends weren't there anymore. In another dream she was wearing a wedding dress but the wedding hall was empty. And in another she was playing with other children. The children were divided into groups but she was left without a group. Indeed, from the moment Valentina began to be aware of her anger, even if she didn't actually express it toward someone, her anxiety started to dissipate. Not only did her dreams change, but her therapist observed that on the couch, in her conscious third level of thinking, Valentina started talking in a different way, freer, more liberated, speaking her mind and, above all, seeming to be less miserable.

Valentina is still overly preoccupied with what her husband thinks of her. Every sentence he utters is anxiously examined and analyzed in an attempt to get inside his head and read his hidden thoughts. Interestingly though, Valentina not only lives her husband's inner world during the day but also at night. She has dreams in which she appears in the form of her husband. Then she sees the world through his eyes and knows exactly what he feels. How does it happen that a person dreams he is someone else? In her home, Valentina says, they didn't speak, they simply felt one another, which is why Valentina can feel the other person as if she were him. What seems hardest for Valentina is to live in her home and her world, and to go out into the world from there. Valentina continues to keep her anger diary, and is practicing speaking her mind and saying what she wants without getting into entanglements with other people.

Valentina says that since she began expressing her anger, even if only in writing, she is less ill, less anxious, and happier. On the couch she sobs far less than at the start of therapy.

Valentina is making excellent progress in therapy just because she is a good student. Her therapist praises her in a way her parents never did, and then she starts to cry – except that now her crying is not from anger.

Improving sex and relationships

Valentina has not told her husband about her orgasm fantasy, and certainly not the homosexual part. Were they to be more open with each other, he would understand how important gentleness is to Valentina, and how she expects him to be tender and gentle with her. Perhaps the husband doesn't need to act differently from what he feels, but this understanding could improve their relationship because Valentina will be better understood by her husband and, just as important, will better understand herself. In every relationship, Valentina does expect the other person to be like her – extremely gentle.

If Valentina would dare to inquire about her husband's orgasm fantasy, she could repay him with the same consideration. Valentina's husband is also very embarrassed about his fantasy. In his imagination, there is a cage of beautiful naked girls tied to the bars with legs open so that their sex organs are exposed to penetration from outside the cage. The husband imagines that he is inseminating them in the way hens are inseminated. He inserts his penis into each one for a short time and then moves on to the next. He sees them waiting excitedly for him and then, with the third or fourth girl that he penetrates through the bars with his penis alone and with no other physical contact, he suddenly feels powerful shudders and comes with loud yells. In bed, Valentina could tell him over and again the story that he loves best, changing the course of the story a little bit each time, and understanding that his control of the girls is the part that drives him wild. Sometimes she will tell him what he has told her, how much he would like to check if there is any difference between one sex organ and another, and how he is searching for the perfect one. Valentina, however, will understand that this story is not only important for what happens in bed. She will notice how hurt her husband becomes when he loses control by having to listen to others, whether in his relationship with her or at work. She will then be able to help him understand a very important part of his emotional world that had previously been hidden from him.

In bed, Valentina's husband will gently caress her the way she likes, and will let her fantasize that she and he are two men or two women. Valentina's pleasure and gratitude will then be boundless, seeing that they derive from a deep acceptance of her inner world in which there is no clear distinction between men and women.

22. TEACHER AND STUDENT

"Luna enters the room like a Girl Scout who has just come home. All love and smiles, modestly dressed, her legs swinging on the tall armchair," her male therapist relates. "She is smiling, she is loving, she really looks up to me. The connection she has created with me is precisely her orgasm fantasy. At the start of therapy, she said that what arouses her most is thinking about a big strong man. This was a non-detailed fantasy that more or less coincided with her admiration of me. Later in therapy, she was able to say with a smile that she had discovered exactly what arouses her. She wants this man to teach her all kinds of new things; that's what really turns her on. This amended fantasy fits her behavior with me even more. Not only does she frequently turn to me as a big father who knows everything, but she does this playfully, with a smile that I also find contagious. I enjoy being with her." Luna grew up in a single-parent family without a father. It is not surprising therefore that her orgasm fantasy dwells overtime on her relationship with her therapist, but not only with him, of course. She did not invent it especially for him. This is how she meets the world. Perhaps it is also not surprising that she once slept with her boss. Afterwards, they went on working together as if nothing had happened.

How did Luna's orgasm fantasy develop? Presumably it developed in her relationship with her mother when Luna was one or two years old, her first and automatic response to her daily reality – her default response. Picture a child who is just starting to walk, maybe can say a few words, and then a marvelous thing happens. Something in him is shaped and crystallized for the rest of his life, the primal bond. Does the child have the power to influence the parent who cares for him or does he feel helpless in relation to him? What does he do with his angers and his fears? An entire rich world in the form of a story with unique characteristics that will only emerge more than a decade later (usually not before adolescence) is then fixed for the rest of the person's life. For Luna, what was fixed was something positive, playful, cheerful. She wanted her mother to teach her new things, which she enjoyed. The same situation could develop with a father figure. The orgasm fantasy that becomes fixed in each of us through the relationship with one or both parents is not exclusive to our relations with one of the sexes. In Luna it developed in her relationship with her mother who cared for her and afterwards was extended to her relationships with the whole world, and now with her therapist in particular.

Luna always expects someone big to teach her enjoyable and interesting things. This is a true lifelong gift. Luna was an outstanding student who always achieved the best grades. Furthermore, everyone around her loves her, including her therapist, because she engages them via her orgasm fantasy. She is always ready to listen to and learn from others. How could they not love her!

Luna's mother describes how she would take Luna everywhere and do everything with her, and how much she enjoyed this. She could be cooking with little one-year-old Luna in her mother's arms peeking into the pots. Her mother explains to her what she is doing and shares her thoughts with her, all with a little laugh. This is exactly how Luna enters the clinic...

Could we guess what Luna dreams about, her first level of unconscious thinking? Not so easily it appears. Her therapist notes a recurrent central motif at this level, namely, a strong Luna saving other people. Once, in an abandoned tower, a bird of prey swooped down on her mother and actually lifted her up in its beak. Luna struggled with the creature, holding on to her mother as strongly as possible, and prevented the bird from snatching her mother away. In another dream a war was on and her mother sent her to bring some medicine for her. There was shooting outside, but little Luna, maybe ten years old in the dream, succeeded in carrying out the mission. In another dream she had to sleep with criminals but managed to get away by making a sad face and they let her go. In yet another dream a tiger (apparently a relative) came to devour her and she persuaded him not to, or else she got him interested in something else and again was saved from disaster.

How do such nighttime dreams develop in a young girl? Friends of hers say that to this day Luna is her mother's mother. From the time she was little, she would caress her mother to comfort her and help her fall asleep and her mother would consult with her about every little thing. Apparently, from her first year of life, Luna sensed that she had the power to breathe life and joy into her mother, and to help her in different ways. This is when the strength and fortitude she would show at a later age took shape. The nature of their relationship continued in this way. Luna's mother tends to join in with her friends as if she is Luna's friend, and the daughter frequently overlooks her mother's behaviors that are not associated with good motherhood, such as when her mother envies her success with guys or gives her foolish advice on other matters. Luna quickly forgives her and keeps her close. Is she her mother's mother or not? ! It's no surprise that Luna was the "class queen." Apparently, these are the types of dreams a "class queen" has, about power and control through struggles. Her therapist senses how Luna fights and wins. How? In her forward-leaning body language, in the way she immediately looks for solutions to problems, in decisively remaining focused on the objective, and in always being imbued with fighting spirit – but with a smile.

What we have been able to ascertain thus far is that Luna generally has a powerful and aggressive dream world in which she doesn't allow herself to feel weak or miserable. In the absence of a father at home, Luna became her mother's mother and essentially missed out on her childhood. On top of that, a pleasant and playful orgasm fantasy was constructed in which she very happily learns from the grownups and lets herself be the little one. Is there a connection between the two levels of thinking? Possibly in her real-life relationship with her mother, which finds expression in her orgasm fantasy, Luna allows herself to compensate for her nighttime experience from the first level of thinking, by letting herself be little.

In the conscious third level of thinking, Luna does not have recurring daydreams. What she does say about herself, and her friends concur, is that she can be highly critical. She doesn't simply speak, she snaps at others. Why? It's not surprising that someone who in her first level of thinking – the dream level – constantly has to be strong, would also be angry and critical towards other people who put her in this situation. It's also not surprising that someone who expects to be the little girl who is admired and taught could be angry in those moments when this orgasm fantasy is not fulfilled. Luna thus frequently criticizes her partner, snapping at him and being agitated, as we noted above. In these moments she is genuinely disappointed and, primarily, angry. Luna found herself a partner who is softer and more anxious than she is, someone whose dream world is quite cold and threatening. He's a good, fairly capable guy, but Luna wants more, to be guided and taught. He cannot compete with her therapist, of course. The therapist receives her admiration and her partner gets her scolding and criticism. The therapist has already told Luna more than once that this is not fair and has also shown her how she addresses him out of her playful orgasm fantasy and her partner out of her conscious, extremely critical third level of thinking. But Luna is attracted to her partner's sensitivity and weakness. Why weakness? Because this is exactly what she is lacking.

What is Luna lacking? We've described Luna's three levels of thinking where we saw much strength, playfulness and criticism, from the deepest to the most overt level of thinking, in that order. But we didn't see much anxiety or weakness, or any self-pity. Is Luna not empathic to herself? Does she allow herself to feel weak? Recently Luna cried, perhaps for the first time since she was a child. It was at a moment when she felt that her therapist didn't understand her. This is not the usual Luna. The usual Luna feels sorry for everyone (in the conscious third level of thinking, in addition to being critical) except for herself. So of course she also feels sorry for her boyfriend. Indeed, Luna's "absent fantasy" is tenderness and empathy in relation to herself, and her therapist needs to try to connect her to these feelings. They are not repressed feelings; they simply don't exist in Luna's repertoire of emotions and behaviors. For the most part they are projected onto the other and attributed to him – the other is a miserable wretch but not her, never. As we have seen, in her childhood Luna could not permit herself to be weak and therefore this emotion doesn't even appear in her dreams. Her therapist says that sometimes his eyes are filled with tears when she is talking casually about different things. She laughs and calls him the weepy therapist. He tells her that these are her tears that she is incapable of shedding. Yes, Luna needs to be connected to her weakness in order to complete the picture of her personality. But she will argue, and rightly from her point of view, that she does not feel weak or frightened. Her dreams show that she is right about this, but not when it comes to what she projects onto others. Then she found a nice guy, connects to his weakness and pities him (when she's not criticizing him). In their relationship, Luna is the strong one, the knowledgeable one, the functioning one. Sound good? Maybe. But don't many of us choose our partner based on the "absent fantasy"?

The doorbell rings. Luna is about to come in, smiling. Her orgasm fantasy will always enter before her...

Improving sex and relationships

Luna wants to be taught new things. "I'm not talking about new theories in physics," she jokes. "Just to come up with all kinds of silly things that we can do to one another. Then when he is the teacher and I'm the outstanding student, it happens faster than I planned. This experience in which there is someone older who teaches me and appreciates my performance just drives me wild." It took Luna's boyfriend some time to understand this. But when he did, he also understood something else – that this understanding applies not only to what happens in bed but to their relationship. This is what she wants from him in countless everyday situations.

What does the boyfriend like? He imagines that he has a harem of women who all serve him and he can sleep with whomever he wants whenever he wants. The boyfriend says that this main story has many accompanying secondary stories. But what they all have in common is the feeling that he is the important one and all the women obey him; this is what does it for him. Now when the boyfriend tells the details of his fantasy to Luna, he again explains that for a moment it's not about sex but about the feeling he gets. Luna understands that it's not just in bed, or rather what happens in bed is just one example from real life. Often, her boyfriend needs her to make him feel he is important, and certainly doesn't need the criticism that comes from her conscious third level of thinking. This awareness of the third level thus teaches Luna what not to do.

Recently, Luna's boyfriend taught her the secrets of his harem. There are many women there but she is the only one he wants to inseminate. He doesn't want her to work hard, which is why he sleeps with other women and then, at the right moment, just before the insemination, he must penetrate her, because inside her is the only place he wants to come. Only she deserves to receive his rare and precious seed. Luna's role in this game is to conduct the entire "chorus" and just as a beautiful concert concludes with all the instruments in coordination, the full pleasure for the two of them must end precisely at the moment of insemination. Luna turns out to be a good and responsible student and can be entrusted with such assignments. Now they lovingly caress each other, Luna tells him the story that he told her, goes into details, describes the women, and seems even more knowledgeable about the secrets of his harem than he is. He listens to the story as if hearing it for the first time. Suddenly Luna starts to come and her boyfriend still waits. Oh, how they laugh. She says it's because of him, that it takes him hours to come with that harem of his. He tells her that when she is "a student," he cannot match her pace. Tomorrow she will again visit the harem but only if her boyfriend allows her to. He tells her that tomorrow he will teach her a new game, "command poker," and she is already excited...

Whenever the boyfriend pictures his harem, and whenever Luna is the outstanding student, they both understand that what they are doing with all this pleasure is not just a game. It's a most serious matter for their relationship.

23. HOWLING LIKE MOTHER

John's male therapist thinks that he has never seen him in his true state. What does he mean by "true state"? It refers to how he looks and feels when he's alone and not concerned with others, and can be one hundred percent himself. The therapist imagines that at such a moment he would see John looking sad or lonely, sitting alone, shoulders sagging, hunched over and depressed. Sometimes, however, he does appear this way in the clinic when he isn't angry and combative.

When John talks about his unconscious first level of thinking, a number of central themes may be discerned. One recurrent theme is the experience of profound loneliness. For example, he was with his parents in a restaurant but they sat at separate tables. His mother started feeling faint and his father had no idea what to do. John was flooded with anger at his impotent father. The therapist asked John why they sat at separate tables, even though both knew the answer; this is how John feels with his parents on a daily basis.

In another series of recurrent dreams, John is guilty. A car is sinking in a puddle of water. John runs to the rescue and saves the family by pulling them out of the sinking car and bringing them to safety. During the rescue a woman who was in the car hurt her hand. John, who has rescued the entire family, is sitting at the side, alone, but also feeling guilty because the woman hurt her hand. The therapist asks why he feels so guilty after having saved a family, and why the minor injury the woman incurred had to ruin it all? John often feels guilty, especially in his relationship with his mother. John's dreams also have an element of humor, a car sinking in a puddle of water for example, quite a feat, which shows that in his daily life John can privately laugh at certain events. Indeed, John feels that his parents are sinking in their nonsense.

In yet another series of recurrent dreams with a paranoid theme, John feels persecuted. For example, he wants to pass through a doorway in his university department. A broad-shouldered guy is standing there blocking the way. John tries to pass, the two collide and fall flat on their faces. Only then does John notice that this is a classmate of his, and he immediately apologizes. "Why didn't you ask him to let you go past?" the therapist asks, correctly making John responsible for his dream world, for dreams reflect one's feelings in everyday life. John ponders the question, but has no answer. Both agree, however, that instead of speaking, John acts, and how difficult it is for him to believe that others will listen to him. In this dream John feels that the world is hostile and finds additional confirmation that he is ultimately always guilty.

Each of these dreams represents a long series of dreams that John brought to his therapy sessions, dreams that reflect loneliness, guilt and feelings of persecution How did John develop such an unconscious first level of thinking? Certainly it is connected to his relationship with his parents, a primal, wordless identification with them, and perhaps even a result of genetics. Why, though, is it difficult to identify these traits in John's facial expressions and behavior? The reason, the therapist discovers, is that whenever John encounters the other, he is already at war because of his orgasm fantasy as revealed below. Anyone who has known John for a while can attest to his noticeable restlessness, mood changes, odd behavior and also, for years, his lack of desire for a romantic relationship. We will hear John describe how he sits at home alone, how he cries and how painful things are for him.

What is John's second level of thinking, his orgasm fantasy? When John enters the clinic, as we know his orgasm fantasy enters with him. He stands in the center of the room and deliberates where to put himself – on the couch or the armchair. He smoothly places his water bottle on the small table between him and the therapist, roughly removes his coat, hesitates for a second and then goes to the bathroom. Somehow the therapist feels threatened. It will take him a few months to get used to this entrance routine of John's and to be more relaxed when it happens. Why would John threaten the therapist? Other patients don't behave this way when they make their entrance and don't take up as much room and time as John does.

John then sits down on the edge of the armchair, his body leaning forward. He looks directly at the therapist and says: "Today you've got to help me!" Often, he will describe how before entering the room, he imagines himself breaking down the door. Why breaking, the therapist will ask. "Because I'm thinking that, once again, you won't understand me." This is how John's orgasm fantasy operates before a single word is spoken. This is our primal relationship through which we encounter the world. Afterwards, the conscious third level of thinking, which is more processed and reasoned, will come into effect.

John fantasizes that he is tying a woman up and whipping her as she howls. These are the howls of his mother, he acknowledges. It's the same voice. Sometimes when he masturbates, he imagines that he is taking the woman forcibly from behind. What these two fantasies have in common is John's control of the woman. The content, as we have said, can change, but not the relationship within the fantasy. John's therapist feels that when John enters the clinic he is flogging him, the therapist, and taking him from behind. This is how John has been coming into the clinic for years, together with his orgasm fantasy. Since John did not invent this fantasy for his therapist, presumably this is the way he encounters many people in his daily life.

How did such an aggressive orgasm fantasy develop? Perhaps it is also related to John's dream world as we shall soon see. For example, John describes how his mother doesn't knock on the door of his room but rather scratches the door like a cat. As if she's not comfortable knocking and disturbing him. This scratching gives John the feeling that his mother is afraid of him which makes him a bad and guilty boy. So the moment he hears this scratching on the door, he is filled with anger and ready to kill her on the spot. Perhaps this was how John's orgasm fantasy was constructed early in his life. When he was around a year old, his mother didn't need to preserve his privacy and knock on the door to his bedroom, but she did convey to him the feeling that he was to blame for a wide range of things – character never changes, after all. A certain sigh or expression is enough to convey to the child the feeling that he is at fault and that there's something wrong with him. Another time, she offered to make him a sandwich for school. John prefers to prepare something for himself, but he lets her go ahead. If he doesn't, he could feel guilty. But then again the anger surges. It's no wonder that when he is flogging a woman in his orgasm fantasy she is howling like his mother, because this is the quality of the relationship she created with him in his early life. She filled him with guilt – a main current in his dreams – which led him to develop feelings of anger in his conscious second level of thinking, his orgasm fantasy. It is, however, not always this possible to see the clear connection between the orgasm fantasy and the primal dream world.

What about his father? As often happens he is more connected to the conscious third level of thinking, because he was less close to his son when he was very young.

In John's conscious third level of thinking, he often feels anxious, sometimes accompanied by severe anxiety attacks. During these attacks, he feels what he calls "detachment." Suddenly he is floating, not there, and experiences himself and his surroundings differently. It's as if he can see himself from the outside, while at the same time experiencing an array of physical sensations such as an accelerated pulse and a cold sweat that give him a terrible feeling of not being in control over himself and what is happening to him. After such a panic attack, he is deathly afraid of the next inevitable attack. These attacks leave real scars in his mind. He remembers their exact dates, how long each attack lasted, what exactly he felt, and so on.

What seems to be the origin of these severe attacks that prompted John to seek therapy? In the course of therapy, the therapist helped John to notice that before every anxiety attack, there was a minute, or more accurately, a second of anger that was repressed and then… a panic attack. John couldn't bring himself to tell his parents or a friend or girlfriend what he wanted and then… a panic attack. In other words, he was unable to express his anger because it made him uncomfortable, which prompted another panic attack. Indeed, when the body does not release anger outward, the anger changes direction and attacks the individual. Anger is thus transformed into anxiety and often depression in which the person also attacks himself (I'm worthless, guilty, etc.). John slowly learned to identify the anger that had eluded his consciousness and had settled into the depths of his unconscious, and would apparently appear at night. As soon as he grasped it he was able to stop the incipient panic attack at the last minute.

Where did this anger come from? It, too, emerges from the conscious third level of thinking. This is not the automatic anger of the orgasm fantasy. Rather, it arises in the wake of some event that aroused anger in John that he was unable to express. Interestingly, these anxieties are not manifested at all in the first two levels of John's fantasies. But the repressed anger may be seen in John's dreams. Recall how angry John felt when his "impotent" father didn't help his mother who was fainting in the restaurant? We can imagine that at some moment in reality John felt very angry with his father for not helping his mother and was unable to express his anger, and then... a panic attack. The same goes for the dream in which John is aggressively trying to pass through the door that his friend is blocking. There too, repressed anger is revealed. John thus demonstrates the connection between the conscious third level of thinking and the unconscious first level and how anxiety and anger – the former directed inward and the latter directed outward – are split between these two levels.

How did John's relationship with his father give rise to such anxiety attacks? John often repeats that he wants a father rather than being his father's father. He perceives his father as weak, resting his head on John's shoulder expecting to be patted. At other times his father just sits, shoulders sagging, detached from his surroundings and sunk in depression. Sometimes, though, the father can be very critical. When John wants to eat, his father calls him a "glutton," and when John knows something his father doesn't know, his father sneers that he's a "know-all." If John has a hole in his shirt, his father will poke his finger in, which is enough to drive a kid crazy. But John doesn't have anyone to get angry with, because he experiences his father as so weak and not someone he can talk to, so that his anger won't lead to anything. John senses that this anger comes from his conscious third level of thinking. "It's not the instant anger I feel about my mother in my orgasm fantasy," he says. "It's a more distant and thought-out anger about how he doesn't function as a father." This could be why John has trouble criticizing a friend in his conscious third level of thinking. In his mind anger is something you repress and don't let out, and this anger immediately turns into anxiety.

John's conscious third level of thinking, however is richer and more varied. Sometimes, for example, John plays what he calls "panda bear." This mainly happens with girls but also with his therapist. In this scene he becomes a cute, sweet fellow, a nice and most importantly, non-threatening guy. He is aware that he plays "panda bear" to conceal his orgasm fantasy that is aggressive toward women and men alike. We thus find here a connection between the conscious third level of thinking and the second level of the orgasm fantasy.

John further demonstrates the connection between the conscious third level of thinking and the unconscious first level of dreams. This happens when John is walking down the street and sees a rowdy group of hooligans. For a fraction of a second he feels threatened and frightened. Then he immediately begins to run a film in his head of how he fights them. The fear, of course, is repressed and disappears into the first level of thinking, the dream that will appear at night. The daydream does not necessarily have a happy ending. John is hurt and others tend to him. People gather around him and say, "Be quiet, John has been through some hard things." Thus, John often has daydreams in which he is injured and others take care of him. This time we see a connection between the first and third levels of thinking. John's fear that was repressed into the first level of thinking spawned the daydream about fighting the hooligans, and since it is hard for John to imagine winning this fight, he pictures a somewhat pleasant scene in which he has been hurt and is being taken care of.

Were John to have a daydream in which he vanquishes the hooligans, he may possibly in real life be less afraid to grapple with difficulties and wouldn't be looking so much for others to pity him and take care of him. For example, he might be less inclined to surrender to his anxieties and not attach so much importance to them. In this respect the daydreams that belong to our conscious third level of thinking are also responsible for guiding our lives.

When John sees the hooligans, he doesn't believe he could overpower them because he doesn't have a father figure that held himself in high regard, nor a father figure that held John in high regard ("the absent fantasy"). For this reason the therapist often finds himself in awe of John. For John is indeed working very well in therapy and it is not difficult to admire him. So when his therapist says to him, "You're great!" or "Well done!" in response to something John said or did, John is moved to tears. John had a dream in which he and his father come to a therapy session so that his father could see how John speaks with the therapist and learn from it. Clearly, John's "absent fantasy" is admiration.

John's hysterical and colorful personality and his high level of self-awareness has enabled us to illustrate the three different levels of thinking and the connections between them.

Improving sex and relationships

For a long time, John avoided becoming involved in a serious romantic relationship because he felt he was too confused to bring someone else into his world. He was frequently attracted to girls who listened to him, "psychologists" as it were, and it never ended well, for the same reason that John's therapist found it difficult to contain his tumultuous world. Recently he met a girl who is somewhat self-absorbed but stable, with her feet on the ground, a banker by profession who isn't willing to let John harp on his feelings. This surely calms him.

They do, however, have a problem in bed. In order for John to get an erection he needs to envision his aggressive fantasies in which he is flogging a woman. He finds it difficult to picture these images while they are having sex. He feels that she sees and hears these fantasies, at which point he is not really with her, which keeps him light years away from his girlfriend in their most intimate moment. He finally mustered up the courage to tell her about his fantasies. "I'm not really whipping," he assured her "and all you have to do is to be an actress, to enrich the world of your experiences and fantasies and participate in my celebration. What do you think?" It took John's girlfriend a while to get over her shock but when she did, a real celebration began. She described to him how he was whipping her and she howled in a way that sounded to John just like his mother. Suddenly he was "as hard as a rock," as he described it. The first stage in improving their sex life culminated in success. John doesn't need Viagra; all he needs is imagination, as does his girlfriend.

John's girlfriend admitted that she doesn't know what her orgasm fantasy is. She can climax when John is inside her but she insists that she isn't thinking then about anything. She decided to approach this question rationally, as if it were a long-term stock-market investment. She put time aside and began masturbating daily, trying out different stories in her imagination to see what would arouse her. Porno movies also helped. One day it happened, and she herself isn't sure how. She just imagined that she was going down on herself and performing oral sex on herself. Yes, she knows this is not possible but in the imagination everything is possible, and this fantasy drives her totally wild. Since she discovered this fantasy she knows that she has discovered something important about herself – a gift for life.

John enters his girlfriend from behind. She sees her vagina and imagines that she is reaching it with her tongue. He is riding her and controlling her from behind, and describes to her how she is pleasuring herself and doesn't need anyone. She just drives herself wild as she goes down on herself. No one in the world can make her feel as good as she herself can, exactly, exactly... She uses her hand, while her other hand supports this whole complex structure. She describes to him how he is whipping her and riding her with all his might. Suddenly his galloping disturbs her concentration... He stops, imagines that he is controlling and whipping and will resume galloping at any moment. Her hand continues to knead, suddenly she is filled with anxiety, a shudder, more anxiety and more shuddering, and then relaxation. She cannot bear any more, she is done, but this actually drives him crazy.

For he must retain control. He knows that she wants him to come quickly now, that for her the game has to stop. Another gallop or two and John feels the orgasm throughout his body. Sometimes it feels stronger than he can bear...

They are lying on the bed, she on her stomach, still in the grip of her imagination, and he exhausted from his galloping. But she knows how patient she needs to be about his aggression and he knows how patient he has to be, knowing that sometimes she doesn't see him and is absorbed in herself. Now as they hold each other and promise one another to remember what they have just learned, sleep carries them away long into the night...

24. A Woman's Hands Beckon To Me

Is it appropriate to describe a person by means of his dream world, rather than how he looks or behaves? I tend to remember my patients on the basis of their dreams, and pay equal if not greater attention to this world than to the details of their real lives. This world is where the results of the translation of reality into our secret language, the language of dreams, is found. Samuel's male therapist proceeded this way as well.

Samuel came to therapy because he was experiencing moderate anxiety. A brilliant scientist who from the start asked his therapist not to laugh and then proceeded to tell him that he believes he will find a drug that will eliminate death and give people eternal life. Not only did the therapist not laugh, but was even rather impressed by Samuel's desire to save himself and humankind, and especially how motivated this charming fellow was to accomplish great things. Even if he never finds a cure for death, the therapist thought, the gleam in his eye should never be extinguished. Besides, with such motivation, Samuel will surely make other discoveries along the way.

The anxieties in Samuel's conscious third level of thinking were easy to address because Samuel and his therapist quickly observed that whenever Samuel doesn't do what he wants to, he feels anxious, which often takes the form of different physical sensations. Whenever he lacks the nerve to refuse a request from a (male or female) friend, or from his parents, a feeling of anxiety immediately envelops him. A "modest" price to pay for his desire to please others rather than express his anger. Where did his anger disappear to? We shall soon discover.

Samuel's special world was revealed when he began to tell his dreams. In one series of dreams a scary doll with green eyes and a screechy voice would visit Samuel at night and place its cold hands on him. Samuel would wake up with a scream and in a cold sweat. It didn't take long for him to understand that this was none other than his mother – the same eyes and voice. In the course of therapy, Samuel's dreams slowly began to change. At first, he was less frightened by the cold hands. Later, he even asked her, albeit in a trembling voice, not to touch him. Later still, for no apparent reason she no longer touched him and only stood next to him. Gradually she moved further and further away, and one time Samuel even dared to look at her directly. In later dreams, he noticed that the doll was approaching him less. He would then hide from her and peek at her from behind the closet. Once he had the impression that his therapist was hiding there with him, and later he also dared to quietly follow her around the house. This continued until one day he yelled at her: "Fuck you!" slammed the door and went out into the street. He had never done this before and this time it didn't happen in the unconscious first level of thinking – in a dream – but in reality.

Dreams do sometimes change in the course of therapy. They are the patient's shadow that is cast on his sleep at night, and perhaps also a reflection of his soul mirror into the night. Samuel, who was scared to death of his mother and therefore did not forcefully stand up to her, which gave rise to his anxieties, gradually began to muster courage and to fear her less and less. The anxieties also gradually abated as he became freer in expressing himself to her.

What is also special about Samuel are his creative dreams of a kind that therapists don't always get to see. Isn't every dream creative? Absolutely. However, for example, Samuel had a dream about how he was building a clock out of living biological tissue on top a high mountain. This biological clock, which we all have, and that is also responsible for the time of our death, was up there for all to see. He describes how the hands of the clock and its numbers that marked the years of our lives were illuminated at night by the light of the moon and the stars. He remembers how he found a way to control the rate at which the hands advanced and to slow them down. Then his father appeared and Samuel extinguished the lights of the clock so that his father wouldn't see them. Why? Samuel says it's because he would surely not be impressed, and would only be critical. Afterwards, his father put him inside a plastic bag and brought him down from the mountain. Samuel recalls that these are the black plastic bags in which they wrap the dead. He did indeed have a fraught relationship with his father. Samuel who wanted to live forever felt that his father treated him as if he were dead. Perhaps this is where his motivation to live forever originated?

In another dream, Samuel went on a long journey through a system of underground caverns only to suddenly emerge at night on top of Mount Scopus in Jerusalem. Suddenly the entire universe was laid out before him and he watched the planets track across the sky. Someone told him there was much more to explore and discover. He directed his gaze at different planets and saw magical worlds where no human had ever set foot. Samuel was filled with tremendous excitement in the dream and again when he related it to his therapist, who along with Samuel also felt very excited and only said to him, "What creative dreams!"

Samuel had many other fascinating dreams. In one, he tried to assemble a puzzle that was a picture of a father and son. Talented as he is, Samuel was unable to assemble the puzzle. This time, however, when he recounted the dream, he and his therapist were almost in tears.

Samuel is a gifted scientist who records his dreams every night. He believes that many ideas of how to solve difficult problems actually surface when using the irrational tools that emerge from the dream world. Thus when he is stuck in a thicket of logical and rational thoughts with no way of escape, he tries to think about the problem at night when he is in the state between sleep and wakefulness, and lo and behold simplicity triumphs. He reminds his therapist that Mendeleev understood the cycle of the elements of nature and came up with the periodic table in his sleep. He dreamed about this order and when he awoke he had the solution in hand. Similarly, Friedrich August Kekule discovered the circular structure of benzene when he dreamed about a snake trying to catch its tail. Many others also achieved great insights in this fashion. In fact, for the most part, Samuel has good dreams in which his abilities are revealed.

What is Samuel's orgasm fantasy? A woman is beckoning to him, her hand signaling him to come to her. Then he comes. "What is the feeling that arouses you?" his therapist asks. "The feeling that I'm a good boy," Samuel replies without hesitation. "That is why she calls me to come to her." Every orgasm fantasy must be explored in order to identify the emotion that it contains. The picture alone is not enough. What matters is how the individual experiences it. Why does Samuel have such an orgasm fantasy? If we think about Samuel's dreams of the scary doll, we realize that it's possibly no coincidence. This was precisely the nature of his early relationship with his mother. He had to be a good boy and please her, she would then signal him to come to her, and then they would be together. Another important piece of information is that Samuel's mother had postpartum depression. So it's quite likely that she didn't pay much attention to baby Samuel who thus wanted to please her even more. Indeed Samuel tries to please everyone – his friends, his wife and also his parents. His default is to be a good boy, to please, to not assert himself; most important is satisfying the other person. In an incredible childhood memory from age seven, he writes a reminder to himself in a notebook to get angry at his parents and not to forget to do this. Of course, he did forget, but he recalled it in therapy. What did Samuel do with all the anger he felt toward his parents over the years? He repressed it and felt anxious. So when you ask Samuel what he thinks about most of the day or what kind of thoughts he usually has, he admits that he goes around with a lot of anger; in his mind he is frequently arguing with and shouting at people, but doesn't dare do so in reality. Indeed, in his conscious third level of thinking Samuel is angry most of the time, and if not angry, then anxious. We see that the displacement of anger can remain in the conscious third level of thinking as happens with Samuel (in which case it might be appropriate to call this a split rather than repression) or it is repressed into the unconscious first level of thinking as we have already seen. And sometimes it may not appear in any level, but simply be projected onto others, as we have also seen. In short, anger may undergo a split, repression or projection.

In Samuel's case, we thus see a clear connection between his three levels of thinking. How at the beginning of therapy, in the unconscious first level of thinking, dreams, he was afraid of his mother and didn't communicate with his father. Then how these relationships gave rise to an orgasm fantasy whose default is about pleasing his mother – as a young boy he was responsible for many of the household chores. It is therefore not surprising that in his conscious third level of thinking he is flooded with anxiety and anger. Lately, as his awareness has increased, his anxiety and anger have decreased and he has become more assertive in appropriate situations.

At the entrance to the clinic, however, Samuel always enters hesitatingly. Why? Is he waiting for the therapist to beckon to him, similar to what happens in his orgasm fantasy? Samuel knows that this is his time and his place; he is not new to therapy. The therapist isn't sure he knows either. Samuel is aware that he is hesitant and says that he is always like this in the beginning no matter where he is.

He then lies on the couch and starts talking about his problems with his wife. For years they've been working on this in therapy – that he shouldn't just aim to please her, but should speak his mind. Samuel reminds the therapist that his orgasm fantasy hasn't changed and that he will just have to live with this situation for the rest of his life. Like someone with chronic heart disease who has to constantly be careful, he says. The therapist then asks him if he dreamed anything during the previous week. Samuel's dreams give him and the therapist much pleasure and strength. Samuel describes another scientific discovery of his and the therapist, who of course doesn't completely understand the significance of Samuel's discovery, still grasps the gist of what he is saying and can't stop exclaiming in awe. Samuel feels that he can continue coming to therapy his whole life because he has found someone who loves and understand him and, most importantly, is always there for him.

Improving sex and relationships

Samuel and his wife do talk about his orgasm fantasy. She knows how careful she needs to be so as not to impose things on him. At first he will consent and seek to please her from his second level of thinking, from his orgasm fantasy, and afterwards he will feel anxiety and anger in his conscious third level of thinking. Familiarity with Samuel's orgasm fantasy has helped them improve the dynamics between them. In bed, Samuel's wife always does whatever he asks. He sees her hands beckoning him and she tells him that he is a good boy, which gives him an incredible erection. He then tells her that he is dying with pleasure.

In her fantasy, as Samuel holds her head on his thighs, she envisions a big muscular man spreading her legs and penetrating her. "It's a bit insulting," Samuel tells his therapist with a little laugh. "I want to be the one penetrating her and not some unknown brute. And all this is happening while I'm holding her head and stroking her. Why?" Samuel's wife says, in all honesty, that it's hard for her to feel attracted to Samuel because he is so small and scrawny, so she imagines big strong men instead. "I know you're a good guy," she says. "You're good for petting but not for sex." Samuel used to be terribly offended by this, but now he just laughs about it. "What do I care what you're imagining as long as I'm the one stroking your head," he says with a chuckle, and then rephrases it – "as long as I'm going crazy with pleasure." Recently, Samuel's wife began to picture that he is penetrating her. This happened after he received an award for excellence in his research. Suddenly he appeared to her as the big strong man in her orgasm fantasy and she felt very attracted to him. Samuel laughs again. Apparently, every fantasy his wife has is good for him. But he just tells her that it's a shame he sometimes has to be not nice to her for her to be attracted to him.

Samuel's wife recently realized that she is able to climax in her orgasm fantasy because Samuel is soothing her with his caresses. Otherwise she wouldn't be able to come. She doesn't know why there are two men in her orgasm fantasy – one who enters her and another who caresses her while that is happening. Her father, she feels, was a rather crude and violent man while her mother was warmer and gentler and often mediated between them and enabled her to communicate with him. Perhaps this is the source of the fantasy. Samuel's wife says she can achieve satisfaction with various stories. In each one, however, there has to be someone who is soothing her and another who is penetrating her. Samuel actually noticed some time previously that his wife needs him to soothe her not only in her orgasm fantasy but also in a variety of real situations in which she finds herself under pressure and feels threatened. For example, she may get into trouble at work for some reason, and will immediately seek someone who can soothe and reassure her. But he also notices that at times she wants him to be almost aggressive and violent, and this duality confuses him.

Now when she shows Samuel her delicate, beckoning hands and calls him to come to her because he is a good boy, Samuel, who until a moment before wasn't in the mood for sex because he was preoccupied with some scientific problem, immediately gets an erection. He sits behind her and places her head on his thighs. Her hands reach back and hold his penis. This is what a good boy gets, she says to him. Samuel still sees the scientific problem facing him but now it is much more pleasurable. He asks his wife to calm down, to relax and let the sexy man freely penetrate her. Samuel's wife shudders just at the sound of these words, as Samuel caresses her head. Then Samuel enters her, and strokes her beckoning hands, but she is there with her muscular man; suddenly she thinks that it's Samuel: "It's you!" she shouts. "It's you there! Amazing!" Samuel is not all that interested in who is there in his wife's orgasm fantasy. Right now he is either picturing her hands or starting to come – at these moments he just doesn't know what is happening to him. Currents of electricity climb from his behind up his back to the top of his head. One day he will investigate this phenomenon of orgasm too, of that he is certain. And what about his wife? She comes before him, and can't understand how she used to find him unattractive. Now she suddenly thinks that every girl who isn't attracted to a guy should sleep with him before she makes up her mind if that is really the case. To just reverse cause and effect. Samuel the scientist likes the idea. He tells her that the idea applies to men too and that she should patent it. His teasing makes her want him to penetrate her again. She'll soothe herself this time...

Later they went to a restaurant, looked each other in the eye, sipped red wine, raised a toast to their amusing orgasm fantasies and swore their everlasting love for one another in the name of these orgasm fantasies that unite them. He requested that she always tell him if she wants him to be caressing or fucking and she admits that she isn't always sure...

25. REMOTE-CONTROL SADIST

Henry is a successful high-tech executive with a number of lucrative exits to his name. He thinks that the driving force to develop new things and cope with big challenges stems from the family conversations around the dinner table since he was little. Over the years, his father, a high-ranking officer in a combat unit, shared with the family his and his comrades' tales of heroism. "It wasn't just the story, it was the spirit of the story and the light in his eyes," says Henry. "Sometimes I would get goose bumps when my father told his heroic tales. But as the years went by, the stories tended to repeat themselves and we children knew them by heart. Still, the spirit always remained."

In his youth, Henry was an excellent swimmer who took part in team competitions, occasionally winning medals. He had a pleasant recurring daydream that belongs to the conscious third level of thinking. He is standing on the podium before a cheering crowd, a gold medal around his neck. Later, when he decided he wanted to be a doctor, this daydream was replaced by another in which he, an eminent doctor who finds a cure for cancer, is awarded the Nobel Prize and receives worldwide acclaim. Henry noticed that the theme of success could change from being a swimming champion to a great physician, and later to other things, but the spirit of success was the spirit of his father's stories that he heard as a child.

In his twenties, Henry decided to seek psychotherapy. He realized that these happy daydreams – the videos he runs in his head at different times – did not appear randomly. These videos would usually start in the wake of a feeling of humiliation, insult or distress that passed through his mind, and whose purpose was to raise his spirits. With the help of his male therapist, Henry understood in these instances that the brief insult had slipped away from him into his nighttime dreams. With his therapist's encouragement, Henry developed a habit: Whenever such a scene plays in his head, he tries to stop for a moment and ask himself: How did it start? What was he thinking about just before the video started running? In this way he learned to identify and even capture the thought before it disappeared into his unconscious. It was always an insult or disappointment that Henry experienced as unbearable. "As soon as you capture the insult and are aware of it, it will no longer appear in a dream," his therapist explained. "This is the essence of the unconscious." Henry thus understood that his brain is completely autonomous and wants to make him feel good. Henry had no doubt that a large part of his high-tech success could be attributed to the uplifting spirit instilled in him in his father's home, a spirit of there's nothing you can't do and no challenge you can't meet. And indeed, Henry often got to see the gleam of admiration in his father's eyes.

Henry's nighttime world, which belongs to the unconscious first level of thinking, was far less simple. He had a main stream of paranoid dreams in which he tried to shoot his enemies but often his weapon didn't work or the bullets had no effect on the enemy. Sometimes he struggled to hold his own in the face of a hostile world, and to assertively speak his mind. It was as if he couldn't even form the words. On other occasions he had to escape, hide, or disguise himself so as not to be recognized.

In another series of dreams Henry is sitting on a high balcony overlooking a spectacular landscape when the balcony begins to give way.

Where did this insecurity come from, everything from menacing people to collapsing buildings? Both Henry's parents had paranoid tendencies, and seemed to have viewed Henry through similar lenses. For example, they would say that they believe everything he says but then check that he was really telling the truth. The child thus absorbed his parents' attitudes toward the world and toward him with no differentiation. One of the biggest insults in Henry's home was to be taken for a sucker. "A person has to make sure he isn't cheated," was his parents' motto.

As for the dreams about the collapsing balconies, Henry noticed that the more he imagined in his conscious third level of thinking the great things he would do, the greater the chance in his unconscious first level of thinking, in his dreams, that things would come crashing down. Sometimes these fears were not even repressed into a dream. In his conscious third level of thinking, Henry sensed that ultimately others would discover that he was really just a loser. He experienced this as a real physical sensation of collapsing inside, and referred to it as "a hole in the stomach." The reason he didn't fall from low balconies but rather from balconies that were very high up and overlooked magnificent vistas was that they were as lofty as his grandiose fantasies from which he would crash down. In short, Henry had two main themes in his dream world: the paranoid theme that related to his encounters with different people in the course of the day, and the theme of collapse that was a reaction to his grandiose plans.

Only when Henry began to write down his dreams did he discover how frightening his inner world was. Before that, he had got used to living with uncomfortable but unidentified feelings. Henry was quite stunned to discover how his inner world looked, and how threatened he felt in it. Previously he would have claimed that, at most, he felt a little uncomfortable at times, even if in his dreams his life was suddenly in danger. If people would regularly write down their dreams, many would discover hidden worlds that they never knew existed. Could Henry's dream world have been detected from the outside? Neighbors and friends would probably have said that Henry was a happy child. This was perhaps the superficial impression of those who saw the gleam in Henry's eye, his zest for life, and his motivation emanating from the conscious third level of his daydreams. Henry was indeed a cheerful child. But a smile often hides fear. Anyone who looked deeper would have observed his restlessness and the attention deficit disorder that plagued him over the years. Sometimes he just didn't absorb what people were saying to him. He may, however, not have been open to it because in those moments he was escaping from an insult into a pleasant daydream. As a child he often hurt himself, was very talkative and asked a lot of questions without waiting for answers, apparently in a bid for attention. All these were clear signs that his inner world was neither calm nor safe.

Henry discovered his second level of thinking, his orgasm fantasy, relatively late, around age thirty. Prior to that he enjoyed sex with women but didn't think he had any special recurrent orgasm fantasy. What bothered him was that, unlike his friends, he couldn't climax with masturbation. It just didn't stimulate him or work for him. However, when Henry did find the fantasy that stimulated him, suddenly he could masturbate and come easily. It became clear that Henry's orgasm fantasy had been repressed because of its unpleasantness in relation to his self-image.

Henry imagines that other men are raping his girlfriend, and that he was actually sending them to do the dirty deed for him. They are big and strong and do what they want to her while he watches. She surrenders to these powerful men because she has no choice, and this is the moment at which he comes. Henry specifically chose men who would humiliate his girlfriend: childhood friends, relatives, and especially men his girlfriend would not have chosen to sleep with. He recruited them all for the sake of his girlfriend's humiliation and his orgasm. Why?

The simple solution is supplied by Henry's mother. She always claimed he was a stubborn child and that she had engaged in endless battles with him over the years. When Henry discovered his orgasm fantasy, it was initially a "novelty" for him and he used the story to achieve sexual satisfaction. It took him years to understand that the story he tells himself in his orgasm fantasy is not so straightforward and contains hidden truths. He was unfamiliar with other worlds beyond his own. "Who knew that not everyone fights with their mother this way?" he told his therapist. Henry slowly began to understand that in his orgasm fantasy he is settling scores with his mother. But he isn't strong enough to do it himself so he recruits other men for this purpose. Perhaps when he was very young he hoped that his father, whom he loved and to whom he was more attached than to his mother, would settle the scores with his mother for him. Later, other men took the father's place and his girlfriends took his mother's place. Henry regretted that he was not the one raping his girlfriend in his fantasy. Why does he need others to do this? He understood that in his self-experience he was too weak to do it. And indeed, in everyday life Henry recreated his orgasm fantasy of feeling that he was a weakling facing those who were bigger and stronger than him. In those moments he did not behave aggressively toward the other person, but instead, as in his orgasm fantasy, he looked for indirect ways to hurt him. Had Henry's mother been annoying but weaker, Henry might have developed an orgasm fantasy that was directly aggressive toward her. Had his mother been stronger than Henry, his aggression towards her may have been eliminated and a different orgasm fantasy would have developed. But Henry's mother tended to aggravate him in various ways and following a confrontation with him would finally begin to show signs of surrender. An indirectly vengeful orgasm fantasy thus developed. Henry would say that if he finds the door closed he comes in through the window. It was not hard for Henry to understand why his orgasm fantasy had been repressed for all those years. It was simply destructive to his self-image. He who in his daydreams makes lucrative exits, finds a cure for cancer, brings honor to his country as a swimmer and so on, actually harbors a large amount of aggression. So he sends other men to rape his girlfriend. But It isn't only his aggression; even worse – it's his puniness. How can he let others do this? Instead of protecting his girlfriend, is this what he does? Letting other men fuck her only exposes his weakness. But apparently his anger at the woman and his desire to take revenge on her are greater than the humiliation he feels of others having sex with her.

The nuances of his orgasm fantasy provided Henry with rich information about the way he conducts himself in the world. His therapist pointed out that he has something against women. But they both understood that if this was part of his orgasm fantasy, it wasn't only against women. Rather, it was his default response in his relations with everyone.

Henry clearly had something against his mother, as could be seen in his dreams. In his childhood she would sometimes disappear, leaving him alone and abandoned, whether at home, in the park, or in other places. Once, for example, he dreamed that he entered his parents' bedroom and saw his father twice

– lying on both sides of the bed – but did not see his mother, as if she didn't exist. Another time he dreamed that his mother had a male sex organ; he evidently experienced her as very aggressive. In yet another dream she appeared as a whore attempting to seduce him. Thus, it is inconceivable that the orgasm fantasy, which indicates a certain tendency in reality, should not leave some residue in a person's dream world.

Does this imply that Henry's father actually raped Henry's mother in order to get vengeance on Henry's behalf? Certainly not. Many people have an orgasm fantasy that obviously did not occur in reality, for example, a common masochistic orgasm fantasy in which they achieve orgasm by being beaten. Many of those who have this fantasy were never beaten, not by their parents, nor anyone else. Apparently, however, they did experience criticism and blame and the brain, as usual, completes the picture.

Henry is a successful guy. We see that even though his first two levels of thinking contain painful fantasies, they are compensated by his conscious third level of thinking. Indeed, his father's admiration, which gave rise to Henry's grand daydreams, has guided him throughout his life and has enabled him to overcome his internal hardships.

Improving sex and relationships

Almost from the start of their relationship Henry told his girlfriend about his orgasm fantasy. He thought it was important for her to know this side of him, even though he is not proud of it. The girlfriend says that it's not hard to see Henry's orgasm fantasy in action. He can be aggressive towards people in an excessive and unpredictable way, she says. The object of this aggression could be a bank teller or some other service provider whom Henry feels isn't doing their job properly. Yet, she says, at other times he can be the kind and accepting savior of the world, as in his daydreams. When she tells him to take out the trash he may experience this as a command. "He doesn't say no," she laughs, "he just doesn't do it." Henry thinks that this is precisely his orgasm fantasy – indirect revenge. His girlfriend is aware that he can easily feel humiliated in their relationship, and that she will then find him ready for war. "Why does it humiliate you to take out the trash?" she protests. "I cleaned the whole house!" Henry thinks it over. He understands what she is saying and just requests her to ask him in a different way to take out the trash; maybe to add a "please" and maybe with a little more respect.

Henry's girlfriend likes to get him angry before they get into bed. She isn't crazy about sex, and usually would be pleased to forgo it. She mostly does it for him. Maybe this is why she is aggressive before they get into bed? Perhaps she also unconsciously wants to anger Henry so that he will realize his aggressive fantasies toward her even more forcefully. They still don't know what her orgasm fantasy is. Henry is happy with her because she allows him to imagine whatever he wants. Then in his fantasy he has her sleep with children and parents, with relatives and friends, and the greater the perversion, the greater the humiliation and the greater Henry's joy. But what about her? She says she doesn't need to climax. Are there women who really don't need sexual satisfaction? Recently they had a serious fight and were about to break up, when suddenly she began to come. She explained that she just didn't care anymore and said to herself – "Why not?" It's intriguing that the relationship seems to restrain her from climaxing while the thought of breaking up releases her. What is happening here? It's as if she must behave in a "decent" way within the relationship but without a relationship anything goes. Does this resemble the dilemma that some women have between being a "lady" and a "whore," and the feeling that the two don't go together? These women cannot achieve satisfaction with their husbands, but only when they have an affair. Somehow in their imagination there is something to lose by "letting themselves go" in the relationship. Henry thinks that only when his girlfriend allows herself to lose control with him will she start to discover her own orgasm fantasy. "To come is to go mad," he explains to her. "You must allow yourself to go mad!" Sometimes in his imagination Henry envisions her drunk or high and then it happens. He already has a few ideas about the direction her orgasm fantasy will take.

26. GIVING THE MOST PRECIOUS THING

Camilla, 40, a radiant and charming librarian, describes a dream world that is simply good. Indeed, such things exist. In her dreams she is courted by Brad Pitt, Marlon Brando and the like, handles all her daily tasks well, and receives many compliments. In one dream her deceased mother, whom she dearly misses, appears, smiling as if everything is all right. Based on my unrepresentative statistics, there aren't all that many people like Camilla; still they do exist and in the dream world anything is possible. Nevertheless, the confidence that Camilla exudes and her mental calm attests to an inner unconscious dream world that is most enjoyable. Her partner says that Camilla can burst out laughing in the middle of the night, dream about having passionate affairs, wake up in the morning with a smile and tell him all that she dreamed. With an inner world like this, who needs reality?

Camilla greets people with a smile, with ease, and gives them her full attention. In her company people who know her feel that all is right with the world. How did such a benign inner world develop? Quite possibly there is a genetic component at work here. But she probably also had a decisive mother who instilled confidence in her and was clear about what she wanted. And a father who was possibly less involved but definitely uncomplicated, a man who also knew what he wanted. There are people who repress anxieties into the unconscious level of thinking and others who repress wishes so as not to indulge in illusions and then to be disappointed. Camilla is of the latter type.

What is Camilla's orgasm fantasy? A surprise awaits us. Camilla climaxes at the same time as her boyfriend. She needs him to come, to gaze at his face contorted with pleasure, and instantly she is there too. Without him, it is difficult for her. So we could say that Camilla is a dependent type. This, however, is only part of the story, because Camilla's most arousing fantasy is of a man who rapes her from behind, who forcibly penetrates her when she isn't prepared for it, and who also hurts her a little. But she immediately adds that she knows she is giving him the most precious thing a man can be given. He is doing to her what he wants, dominating her, raping her, but she is there for him, giving to him, becoming one with him and, as we said, climaxing along with him. If so, is it rape? Talking about it, Camilla corrects herself. She understands that it isn't exactly rape, but she immediately amends that as well by saying that she wants him to rape her. We thus see that the complexity of the nuances of the orgasm fantasy has no limit. Is Camilla's orgasm fantasy also evident in her everyday life?

Camilla lives with her boyfriend. She always thinks in terms of two people; she thinks about the home they share. It seems she also thinks about him before she thinks about herself in everyday life. She does the shopping and cleans the house. She does get mad if he makes a mess and doesn't help out, but she will first do everything for him as if he and she are one and the same. At other times she will immediately blame herself, often unjustifiably. "I did it!" she will often say, even though she didn't. If the car got dented pulling out of a parking spot, Camilla is sure that she did it. Her boyfriend laughs – "It was me," he says and she has a hard time believing him. When something unfortunate happens, Camilla will feel sorry for the people close to her before she feels sorry for herself. For example, when she recovered from an operation with serious complications, in those tough moments she said she wasn't thinking of herself but rather about her poor boyfriend who had to see what she was going through and how painful it must have been for him and how he might have ended up alone. She even thought, if she could, that before she died she would find him another girlfriend who would be good for him. She offers a rationale for this too, namely that the person who dies feels no pain, while those who are left behind and grieve are the pitiable ones. A sensitive observer would notice how Camilla continues to live her orgasm fantasy in many events throughout the day.

When Camilla meets students in the library, some of whom can be real pests wanting her to do all the work of searching for material while they do nothing, the first thing she does is to look at them with her big eyes, really being with them, and giving them her full attention. In her view they say very interesting things. Only later will she perhaps pull back and set boundaries. She's certainly not stupid. A person who meets her feels that he is meeting someone who is really attuned to him. At that moment are the people raping her while she identifies with them, participates with them, justifies them? Possibly. Not physical, rather mental rape. She is there for them, not from the position of a victim but rather as someone who is giving them something very precious. Camilla's warm inner world, combined with her orgasm fantasy in which she wants to give her partner something most precious, has made her someone who is open and good at listening to others.

How did Camilla's relationship with her mother, which created in her a stable and secure unconscious level of thinking, also create a second level of thinking that included an element of self-denial? Many people would describe Camilla's mother as bossy. Because of this, at the stage when her young child is dependent on her, she gives her a sense of security. But from age one or two when the nature of the relationship changes, the baby demands more independence, and speech and games enter the picture, the mother then decided many different things for her daughter. For example, she was very strict about what Camilla could eat and what her daily schedule would be. When it came to food, the mother's control of her daughter was very clear: She insisted that she not eat sweets when her friends were doing so, she forced her to eat healthy foods and essentially controlled everything that went into her mouth. Was her mother raping her? In a certain sense, yes. But Camilla, who had such a stable inner world, understood, with good reason, that her mother wasn't really against her but rather concerned about her, and she identified with what her mother was doing. So what we have here is rape together with a desire to give the rapist what he wants and to identify with him.

As an adolescent, Camilla tended toward anorexia and continued to experience conflicts around food throughout her adult years. How can such self-harm be understood? Camilla says that she feels a high whenever she makes up her mind to overcome her hunger and refrain from eating. At these moments she identifies with her mother's control over her body, adopts it and behaves like her. This pleasant masochism makes Camilla especially attuned to others even at times when this is not easy. Indeed, many pathologies also have a positive side.

In Camilla's conscious third level of thinking, another surprise lies in wait. Camilla is highly critical of others, as the people who know her will attest. When her boyfriend tells her about an argument he had with someone, she automatically takes the other person's side, which leaves her boyfriend deeply hurt. The boyfriend eventually came to learn that this situation also had a positive side to it: It enabled him to see what he previously had trouble seeing – the other person's side of things.

This critical side of Camilla's, which seemingly does not jibe with her orgasm fantasy, comes from a higher level of consciousness – the conscious third level – that tries to be more logical and objective. During her relatively rare moments of stress, Camilla's boyfriend describes how her criticalness turns into self-criticism, at which point Camilla can be ruthlessly cruel to herself, accompanied by feelings of worthlessness and having done horrible things, even when the boyfriend thinks they are trivial and mundane. At these moments, Camilla regresses from the conscious level of thinking to the level of her orgasm fantasy in which she behaves as if she deserves punishment. Aren't these episodes of self-flagellation the emotional equivalent of those of self-starvation? Apparently so.

How did this highly critical conscious third level of thinking develop? Camilla grew up in a demanding, critical family, surrounded by people with a very firm political ideology. A rigid ideology isn't open to different voices. Theirs is a strict moral universe in which right and wrong are as plain as day. This is the atmosphere that Camilla imbibed at home. It's thus no wonder that in her conscious level of thinking she is critical, mainly toward others. Camilla's conscious level of thinking may be understood as a reaction to her orgasm fantasy level – anger about submitting and being hurt. Or perhaps the opposite – she is critical so that others will repay her in kind and fulfill her orgasm fantasy. In many instances, we encounter a masochistic orgasm fantasy level while the conscious level shows an opposite tendency, in this case not sadistic but highly critical. In Camilla's case, the simplest explanation is that her highly critical family and environment shaped her conscious third level of thinking with a dominant judgmental component.

What does someone who encounters Camilla experience? An anxious partner might initially experience the confidence, stability and vivaciousness that she exudes from her unconscious first level of thinking. A deeper familiarity would probably convey the feeling that Camilla is there for that friend, male or female, fully attuned to them, giving, ready to devote herself to them. This is Camilla's response from the default relationship of her orgasm fantasy. As the relationship evolves and becomes more complex, gradually a more critical tone will emerge from Camilla toward her interlocutor. Then, rather than identify with the person she is with, Camilla may identify with the position of someone else with whom her partner is in conflict, or with the system. Sometimes Camilla's outlook will be so balanced as to be painful, because most of us naturally tend to justify our position and that of the people close to us.

This case raises the question of whether the source of various eating disorders could be traced to a masochistic orgasm fantasy? This is certainly a question that can easily be explored. From the author's experience, suicidal tendencies may also be connected to a masochistic orgasm fantasy. Generally, there appears to be a correlation between different types of orgasm fantasy and various psychopathologies. (See afterword on Diagnostics and Pathologies).

Improving sex and relationships

Camilla and her boyfriend have a problem. She wants him to take the most precious thing she can give him, to come from behind and take her without her permission, to surprise her. But he wants her to beg for it: this is what does it for him. When he sees her pleading incessantly for him to sleep with her, his erection flourishes. In bed she doesn't want to ask; she wants a man who will do to her what has to be done. He asks her to beg, just a little, not that much – what's the big deal? Just a little drooling will do, he says to her jokingly. But then it won't be a surprise, she protests. They decide to split, each with their own fantasy and maybe they will meet somewhere at the height of pleasure. Camilla lies on her stomach. Suddenly she feels him penetrating. She isn't ready and it's just wonderful. A little painful but amazing. She turns her face, she wants to see him suffering – suffering from the pleasure she is giving him. The boyfriend, before penetrating, had fantasized that she was begging and pleading, saying she would give him anything he wants if he would just enter her, just come inside her. When he sees her this way, it's hard for him to refuse. He agrees to do her a favor, and feels that he is a really good guy. They sleep together. In his mind she is still pleading, still begging for more, while in her mind he is taking what he wants, without asking questions, like a man. Suddenly he starts to come. How long can he sustain such pleasure. She needs another minute, not so fast, she isn't ready for him to come just yet. He may have come already, but he keeps going for her sake. After all her pleading, now it is her turn. She closes her eyes and sees his face contorted with pleasure, and now she can't hold back anymore either...

Sprawled next to one another, he seeks her hand. He strokes her and she tells him to stop; it really has been too much. She reminds him that it's difficult for her sometimes not being able to say things firmly, and to tell him precisely what she thinks from her conscious third level of thinking in which she is not begging. He, the king, only wants to be asked for things constantly and to be asked nicely. It's not easy to live with a king this way. He knows that she is right. Just a minute before he experienced the proof that she was right in the form of his tremendous and undeniable pleasure. He is aware that sometimes he doesn't do things that he should just so that she will ask him again, that she will beg him. Ultimately he will agree. As he caresses her, he promises yet again that he will be more mindful and that he understands she shouldn't have to beg all the time as in his orgasm fantasy. Speaking from her critical conscious third level of thinking she tells him that he has already promised this a thousand times. He says that with each promise he improves a little, and that she is again being critical. She knows that he is right…

Camilla's boyfriend benefits from her first two levels of thinking, the stability and warmth from her unconscious level and the willingness to sacrifice for him from her orgasm fantasy level. As she criticizes him from her conscious level of thinking, he reminds himself that nothing is perfect, which applies to him too, of course. His awareness of Camilla's different levels of thinking and their characteristics certainly helps him to accept her criticism.

1. CHILDISH SEX

Benjamin, a 25-year-old unmarried patient, says that he is attracted to women but has no sexual fantasies about them. He can have sex with women when he is the dominant one – entering from behind, holding them tightly, and telling them what to do. This arouses him. He does, however, have highly arousing sexual fantasies about men. In his fantasy there is no physical contact. He becomes aroused by seeing that other men are aroused by him. All he has to see are their yearning gazes, their eager eyes, and then, he suddenly has an orgasm. For example, once he was sitting at the beach when a guy came up to him and asked: "How much does it cost?" "Why?" he asks his male therapist excitedly, even though he had no interest in the offer. In the wake of that incident, Benjamin discovered his orgasm fantasy. When he is with people he is conscious that he places himself so that others will notice him. "Something in my awareness of my movements makes other people notice me," he says. That way I immediately identify who is turned on by me." Regarding his relationship with his therapist (transference), he admits that he has also tried a few times to arouse him sexually so that he himself would be aroused. For instance, he once started to tell his therapist what a beautiful dick he has; another time, he spoke excitedly about his past homosexual experiences and described them with much relish. "I'm a guy who's averse to physical contact," he says. "I'm definitely not into blow jobs or penetration, not even kissing. It's the other guy's excitement about me that does the trick." Benjamin adds that he would like to live with a man, but without physical contact and without sex. "A childish kind of excitement is enough for me," he admits. "Essentially, I want the close friend I never had."

We see that, in his way, Benjamin controls women and men alike. Women he takes forcibly from behind, and men he furtively causes to become aroused, thereby controlling them. Throughout this book we see cases of people with bisexual tendencies who have identical relations in their orgasm fantasy with both men and women. Although the orgasm fantasy for heterosexuals is directed at the opposite sex, it is representative of the default relationship with both women and men. This tells us that one part of the "equation" is repressed, an orgasm fantasy that contains similar emotional relations to members of our own sex as we have to the opposite sex. As with Benjamin, people with bisexual tendencies reveal this secret to us. This is an important statement we shall return to on several occasions.

As reflected by the anxiety content in Benjamin's dreams, his story is quite poignant. In one recurrent childhood dream, other children are harassing him in the street while his mother watches from a window and does nothing. When we recommend that people write down their dreams in order to identify central currents in their personality (despondency, guilt, aggression, loneliness, etc.), we pay special attention to recurrent dreams, if there are any, which reveal a particularly prevalent tendency. In another dream, burglars enter his house and tie him up while his mother and father carry on watching television and don't even notice. He also had a dream in which he encounters a lion on the street where he lives, and his mother who is busy hanging laundry doesn't notice or simply ignores what is happening. We understand that Benjamin's inner world is very threatening and that he is alone facing the threat. Furthermore, many of Benjamin's dreams over the years are connected to his family. Clearly, he has yet to disengage himself from them as would be expected of a mature young man on his way to start a new life of his own.

As is true for all of us, Benjamin's dreams express the deepest and most authentic story of how we really experience the world. Benjamin also sometimes talks about various everyday matters with profound panic in which it's not difficult to see the inner threat he feels. He might recount a snub from a professor at the university or a reprimand from his boss, and how these left him completely shaken. To him, at that moment, he encountered a lion. Indeed, the general tendency of a person's dream world may be apparent to the sensitive observer.

In Benjamin's conscious third level of thinking, he emphasizes feelings of depression, self-blame and a sense of worthlessness. There is no further need to elaborate on the nature of his relationship with his parents. Both his unconscious first level of thinking, his dreams, and his conscious third level of thinking, indicate this clearly. They never lie. To sum up Benjamin's emotional world, we can say that both his unconscious level of thinking and his conscious third level of thinking are cold and cruel. Perhaps his orgasm fantasy in which others see him and are aroused by him is Benjamin's developmental response to the experience of his nighttime dreams in which his parents don't see him.

Throughout his childhood, his mother was highly self-involved. She would ask him with a seductive smile: "How do I look?", showing him a new outfit, makeup, lipstick or nail polish. We can assume what happened at the critical age between one and two when the orgasm fantasy is shaped for life. Benjamin would be standing in the playpen. His mother comes to show him her new blush and asks him, "How do I look?" The baby responds with excitement, with a smile, with physical energy. His mother is paying attention to him, she sees him, which, as we know from his dreams, doesn't happen all the time. It's true that she saw him for her narcissistic needs, but she did see him. One could say that she provided him with a mirror image of her own wish, and therefore he became like her. At that time, in the second year of his life, when his mother gave him attention, he felt very excited, and later when he is noticed as an adult he can achieve the same excitement, but this time through sexual satisfaction.

To this day, Benjamin essentially sees his mother as a queen and longs for her gaze. She now has dementia but he cares for her devotedly, recording her words and making sarcastic comments as he says in order to extract from her some hint of recognition.

Benjamin's description of his father has sexual overtones: "What a handsome man he is!" – reminding us of the absent repressions in the homosexual experience that create a heterosexual personality. Benjamin talks about a cold and remote father who is ashamed of his gentle and delicate son. It's no wonder that Benjamin wants a close friend, the kind of friend he never had, someone he can identify with.

It's not surprising that Benjamin yearns for attention from the people around him, be it affection, admiration, respect or any other positive attitude. He is obsessed with gaining the attention of the people close to him, and he gets terribly hurt when he is repeatedly rejected because there is something off-putting in his childlike way of attention-seeking. He keeps obsessing about them, consciously and unconsciously trying to provoke them into relating to him by being nice to them, coming to them with different new offers, asking for favors, offering to be of help – all in the wake of the orgasm fantasy that has shaped his life. One thing he is incapable of doing is to focus on himself rather than on others. In the course of therapy, Benjamin's awareness of his orgasm fantasy and the type of relationships he encourages and creates as a result of the fantasy has gradually helped him to become less dependent on what everyone around him thinks and how they relate to him.

Benjamin's story demonstrates how a heterosexual male identity develops. The child who, at an early stage, may be sexually aroused by his father, represses these feelings and identifies with the father during the Oedipal stage with a sense of masculine brotherhood because he imagines that in this way he will obtain a woman just like his father did. This developmental scenario is the basis for relationships among males that are represented in the conscious third level of thinking. Thus, for example, identification with the flag and the national anthem (possibly even to the point of tears), being comrades-in-arms, calling each other "bro", all represent love in which the sexual aspect has been repressed. Benjamin, who longs for a close male friend and is also sexually excited by the prospect, apparently became stuck at an interim stage, and is attracted to women, but not as much as to men.

Freud maintained that we are all bisexual to start with, and Benjamin, like many others, corroborates this theory. For many of us, an orgasm fantasy connected to someone of the same sex is repressed, but it may still appear in dreams, sometimes in our conscious thoughts or in sexual games during the latency period (age 6-12) in which we simulate intimate relations with someone of the same sex within a group of equals as preparation for heterosexual relations in adolescence. It is also worth noting that there are currently dozens, perhaps even hundreds of different definitions of sexuality, enough to provide an endless spectrum of personal experiences that touch on the sexual identity of each and every one of us. The orgasm fantasy, which tells the personal story of human sexuality, apparently presents an unlimited number of possibilities.

Improving sex and relationships

Benjamin is highly embarrassed to meet men and women because he thinks that his orgasm fantasy which doesn't include actual sexual relations, is very childish and quite unacceptable. His therapist tries to tell him that it is only a fantasy and that no orgasm fantasy is superior or inferior to any other. He, the therapist, can certainly picture a man or woman who would love Benjamin irrespective of his orgasm fantasy. Moreover, they could also understand the meaning of his fantasy and how much he yearns for recognition from others, and even help him with this.

Benjamin recently fell platonically in love with a male friend who is completely unaware of Benjamin's feelings. He fell in love with him because the friend looks at him with passion, just the way he likes. On the one hand, Benjamin seems to be completely in love, while on the other, he can observe himself from the side and laugh about it. Such is the relation between the second level of the orgasm fantasy and the conscious third level of thinking.

Benjamin may also choose to live with a woman. He hasn't yet decided. His desire for children may tip the scales in favor of a relationship with a woman, even though he would feel less sexually attracted. Whatever his decision, his familiarity with his orgasm fantasy will help him in his relations with both women and men.

Benjamin recently met a woman. He is less attracted to her than he is to men, but she so beautifully narrates his orgasm fantasy to him, vividly describing how everyone is staring at him and desiring him, that it makes their sex life especially exciting and pleasurable. Benjamin says that what nature didn't give him, a strong attraction to women, is more than made up for by fantasies, and he's sorry he didn't know this when he was younger.

2. I AM LIKE A BOY THOUGH NOT IN THE FORM OF A BOY

R otem will help us to distinguish between the orgasm fantasy and daydreams, and the orgasm fantasy and nighttime dreams. People do not choose their mates solely on the basis of their orgasm fantasy, be it homosexual or heterosexual. Often, attraction from the conscious third level of thinking is stronger. For example, a man with a homosexual orgasm fantasy may have romantic daydreams about women. These are layers of thinking that were built in different stages of development. This man wants a romantic relationship with a woman and maybe also a family and children because he identifies with these ideas socially, not sexually. He may therefore compromise and forgo fulfilling his orgasm fantasy in favor of fulfilling his conscious romantic thoughts of marrying a woman and having a family.

A male friend told Rotem that every time he comes to visit her, he always encounters her mother first. Rotem, note, is forty years old. When he wants to go to the bathroom her mother suddenly appears to turn on the light for him. He then finds himself sitting in the little bathroom and feeling that the walls are transparent. Rotem asks her male therapist if he realizes how intrusive her mother is. This isn't all. Rotem's mother will ask Rotem to tidy her room for the guest, in the guest's presence, and finally will serve them both delicious cheesecake. Rotem's therapist asks her why she arranges to get together with friends at her parents' home when she has an apartment of her own.

The therapist describes Rotem as having an athletic appearance, and usually dressed in sweats and sneakers. Her face is somewhat masculine looking, her light hair is cropped short and her movements are decisive. "What is your earliest memory?" the therapist asks. Rotem thinks a while and recalls that she wanted her father to take her for a ride in the car but he refused. This was around age three; already then she was disappointed with her father. Rotem's therapist knows that we all have countless primal memories, but generally retain those that have emotional meaning for us. She remembers a few years later how she cried when a friend's mother brought her and the friend to kindergarten on the first day of school and left them there. The therapist notes how painful it is to separate from a parent on the first day of school, and here she needed to separate not from her own mother, who didn't take her to school, but from the friend's mother. Rotem goes on to describe how distant her mother was from the time she was young, busy with her job as manager of a bank. Rotem is the eldest child in the family and has two younger brothers. She described how she played with the boys in her class and very happily ran wild with them as a tomboy.

"Whenever I came to my mother for some affection, she was always busy. To be honest, I was scared of her. When my ball was stolen again I was afraid to go home. I wanted to hurt myself so that my injury would lessen my mother's anger at me." Rotem also remembers how as a child she acted wildly once and broke several things in the house. Her mother hit her and Rotem swore she would never talk to her mother again. But she also remembers how quickly she forgot her vow and did talk to her. The therapist was less impressed by the physical blows than by the childhood memory in which the child cannot continue being angry as she wished to, and how Rotem remembered so well having to forgo her anger that apparently found expression in her forceful body language. The anxiety, however, remained in her conscious third level of thinking.

Rotem describes her father as a "quiet, introverted, almost apathetic" person. The therapist notes "apathetic" as this is the feeling she conveyed. "But when you need him, he's there," she adds. Friends who come over tell her that he doesn't look up from the newspaper to say hello. He only responds if spoken to. This was not a father who could counteract the mother's personality.

"When I was fourteen I had a dream in which I saw both my parents as old people in wheelchairs. From that night onward, I couldn't detach myself from them. I didn't go on field trips or to camp and I couldn't leave home." The therapist thinks that it's unusual to come across a patient who is so cognizant of her unconscious first level of thinking, of her dreams, and who behaves accordingly – in this case in accordance with her anxieties. Indeed, Rotem did not internalize her parents in a way that would have enabled her to separate from them in adolescence. "My mother and I started psychotherapy that led to a complete turnaround in her. Since then, she is like a bottomless container that has all the room in the world for me. I too have less fear and a greater desire to share things with her." The therapist, however, has some reservations about the description of the extreme change. "With hard work, we change a little, and slowly," he tells her, adding that he is sorry to have spoiled her idealization of what happened.

In high school, Rotem, who excelled in long-distance running, struggled to go to training camps, fearing that she would be alone there. Once at camp, however, she would form extremely close friendships with the other girls and find it very difficult to part from them when the camp ended. She once fell in love with a boy and suffered a painful rejection. There was also a boyfriend with whom she had sex but it took her until now to realize that she didn't really love him. Then Rotem fell in love with a girl. At first it disgusted her and she was afraid of the feelings aroused in her. The girl also hurt Rotem's feelings several times and she felt jealous. "I felt that something was wrong with me. Like it's not normal but it's so good!" When she told her mother about this infatuation, she replied that Rotem probably just hadn't found the right guy yet. The therapist thinks that this is practically a (perhaps unconscious) self-fulfilling prophecy.

What kind of mother reacts so calmly to such news?! The therapist noted that the child's name, Rotem, is a unisex name. Perhaps, therefore, it was not particularly difficult for Rotem, as she described it, to come out of the closet and admit her sexual attraction to girls. "It was a destructive relationship that lasted three years," she says, describing her first sexual relationship with a girl without much emotion. "She was like my mother; she did whatever she wanted. It was all there: rejections, breakups, make-ups, with affairs in the middle as well as crazy romantic gestures." Is Rotem fighting to get her mother back? The impression is that in her unconscious first level of thinking and her conscious third level of thinking, Rotem creates relations of deep dependence with a variety of significant figures, and that possible separation from them arouses profound anxiety in her.

Rotem felt that if she didn't break up with this girlfriend, she would be lost. At the time she had a dream. In her backyard she saw a female figure standing with her back toward her, a girl with gleaming wavy black hair. "I felt that this was my partner. When I woke up, I knew that someone else was waiting for me." The dream, Rotem says, helped her to end her sick relationship once and for all. In reply to the therapist's question of whether the gleaming wavy black hair reminds her of anyone, she immediately confirms that it's like her mother's hair. "My current girlfriend also has hair like that." This is the second time, the therapist notes, that a dream of Rotem's changes the course of her life, this time for the better. Rotem ended the relationship and went to Paris to study physiotherapy. During her time there, she had lesbian relationships with a few warm and maternal women. Rotem's lesbianism is probably linked to a quest for a mother figure. Because this figure seemed to be unattainable, it became eroticized.

Rotem's dream world contains several main currents. One of them is that every member of her family dies in one dream or another. "My little brother fell from a ship and drowned. I tried to save him but he was dragged down to the depths. In another dream, I am driving with the same brother up a steep mountain road when suddenly the car slips down over the slope. I understand that I'm about to die, and not just any death, because even if I survive the fall, hundreds of crocodiles with gaping mouths are waiting for me below. Then I woke up in a terrible fright." Rotem relates numerous dreams about falling that express the obvious, how much she fears falling and crashing within herself, and how unstable her emotional world feels. And the death part? This expresses separation, her separation from life, and her separation from other family members. What kind of inner world is Rotem living in, one in which there is no one to hold on to? Once she and her family were staying at a hotel in the desert. She didn't see any figures there; her family were all faceless and there was no communication. Again she was alone.

Rotem also has a series of sexual dreams, "about girls", she says, not boys, in which I am the initiator, the one who is attracted, while my partner is a soft and seductive figure who exudes eroticism. I'm like a boy though not in the form of a boy." The therapist tries to understand better. Rotem says she appears in the dream as herself, as a girl, but knows that she is a boy. She basically behaves and feels like a boy. "Like I was always a tomboy," she adds. Rotem's therapist thinks he is beginning to understand the depth of the experience of being in a body that doesn't match ones feeling of oneself. But Rotem immediately adds that there are aspects of her femininity that she loves and wouldn't want to give up. Therefore, she has never considered a sex-change operation.

Rotem talks about the development of her orgasm fantasy. As an adolescent it was a regular fantasy that appeared during masturbation, in which an active man was penetrating her. Gradually, her point of view changed and instead of seeing the man through her eyes, she began seeing herself through the man's eyes. At a later stage, she not only saw herself through the man's eyes, but she became the man who usually was sleeping with a submissive woman. Along with these changes, which were slow and unfolded over several years, she began to increasingly accept herself. Her body movements began to take on a more masculine and sharp character, rather than the more rounded feminine kind of movements she felt she had been faking her whole life. "That wasn't me," she says with a sigh. Redemptive liberation arrived. It wasn't just the physical movements, it was the change in attire and manner of speech that freed me from the enslavement of living as a feminine figure who isn't me. As the male figure, I am active, I pleasure my partner with cunnilingus, I hold her tight, and I penetrate her with a strap-on penis in both the masturbation fantasy and in reality. But in recent years, another interesting change has begun to develop." She smiles, possibly getting used to this journey of change. "I picture two similar men in a homosexual relationship. Both are strong and active: anal penetration, licking around the anus, but no sucking. An effeminate man doesn't do it for me. I want a macho man." And she, Rotem, identifies with the macho man who is penetrating the other. "Not painful, not sadistic," she qualifies, "but a forceful fuck," she adds, and her therapist admits he was blushing. "I don't like caresses, I like it aggressive. I'm not the one who submits, I'm the one who penetrates."

Rotem underwent a dual journey in order to discover her true orgasm fantasy, in the course of which she changed from being a woman to a man, and the partner figure changed from being a man to a woman and back to a man. Once she overcame the repression, Rotem discovered her orgasm fantasy, which helped her to realize who she really is. For her, and for many others, this is a crucial stage, without which self-realization is impossible, but rather only a life of phoniness and concealment. Rotem is surrounded by complexity. In her dreams she appears as a boy in the form of a girl and is attracted to women, while in her orgasm fantasy, she is a man who is attracted to another man.

She also has many daydreams. In one she is in a race, and with the last of her strength she overtakes the other runners and comes in first. The crowd roars. She stands on the winners' podium facing the cheering crowd. When she feels pre-race anxiety, she automatically activates this victory movie that really helps her. She doesn't need her therapist to explain to her that these movies originate in repressed anxiety that may surface at night. As an outstanding athlete she understands this better than he does. The therapist only adds that this is also the healthy force that pushed her to separate from her family and go to Paris to study physiotherapy, and it is also the force that pushes her to succeed as an athlete. We thus see that Rotem's conscious third level of thinking includes severe separation issues and anxieties, and now also triumphant daydreams.

Rotem has succeeded in creating above her painful and shaky layer of dreams that represents her primal relationship with her parents, an orgasm fantasy with more power and aggression, and with which she encounters the world. Rotem knows that she can be intimidating. At get-togethers with friends, she is usually the leader, the one who takes the initiative and the responsibility, and is respected for it. Rotem's therapist is not surprised. This is how he perceives her in the room, strong and authoritative. Rotem's mother did not create a warm and close bond with her daughter, as Rotem's first and third levels of thinking testify. But during the critical period in which the orgasm fantasy is imprinted, her mother apparently provided her with the ability to dominate and be in control. Possibly, during that critical period, she responded to the baby's needs and perhaps also conveyed a feeling of surrender to the baby's demands, because in Rotem's orgasm fantasy, she seems to want to make her partner surrender to her. In this case as well, we should bear in mind that Rotem has an aggressive orgasm fantasy in relation to both men and women. As we've said previously, our default response to the world is always the same.

Rotem does, however, experience moments of collapse in which she admits that she would like to commit suicide.

She becomes filled with anxiety that everyone will leave her, at which point the defenses of the orgasm fantasy and the conscious third level of thinking break down, and Rotem crashes into her frightening dream world. For example, her athletics coach is an aggressive person who often speaks to her crudely, which causes her to clam up. She then feels a hole in her stomach and that everything is collapsing, perhaps like the collapse in her dreams, she says.

Rotem is romantically attracted to women in both her conscious third level of thinking and her unconscious first level of thinking, her dreams. In many cases the dream is simply a stream of associations that were repressed from the state of wakefulness, and possibly the opposite, conscious thought is simply a stream of thoughts that were liberated from repression. This identity, therefore, is not surprising. In this context, however, the orgasm fantasy is different by being a special fantasy that develops during a critical period in life and needn't match content from the first or the third levels. Rotem continues to have lesbian relationships, even though in its final formulation, her orgasm fantasy is directed at men. This situation is typical of many people whose orgasm fantasy does not match their romantic thoughts at night or during the day, and who have to choose between the two.

Rotem's therapist knows that she needs him as a warm and loving parent. He also knows that her orgasm fantasy will not change. But he believes that Rotem can have a very good life filled with personal choices.

Improving sex and relationships

The complexity of Rotem's thinking at the different levels requires her to be aware of her different tendencies. Does she choose to be with a macho man as in her orgasm fantasy? Or does she choose a feminine figure as in her world of dreams and in wakefulness? Does she choose to see herself as a woman or as a man? Perhaps at different times and contexts, she can adopt different roles in accordance with her feelings, and to continue enjoying her feminine side, even though, during sex, she experiences herself as a man. Rotem can be who she is. But in order to be herself, she has to listen carefully to her three levels of thinking, for that is where her truth lies. Then and only then can she be more attuned to her partner, male or female. As we have said, there is no good or bad orgasm fantasy. There is only awareness of fantasies and lack of awareness.

Recently, Rotem has a girlfriend. When they sleep together, Rotem imagines in her orgasm fantasy two strong and muscular macho men. She, Rotem, aggressively enters her partner. The girlfriend meanwhile imagines Rotem as a warm and good mother, not at all in keeping with her aggressiveness. The way the girlfriend sees it, Rotem is taking care of her, looking after her and wanting her to be happy, which makes her come. The two girlfriends talk about their different natures that is so clear in their orgasm fantasies and how they approach the world in such opposite ways. Rotem is strong and a leader and her friend is gentle and warmer – at least in their immediate responses to the people around them.

Rotem thinks that she can live with her girlfriend even though the girlfriend's gender doesn't fit Rotem's orgasm fantasy, especially because she has a developed imagination and does what she wants with it. For her, Rotem says, this is the real meaning of love, when each woman encourages her partner's fantasies.

PARENTAL GUIDANCE

1. The King

Hugo comes for parental guidance because he feels his young son is controlling him. "I don't want to be his servant," he protests, "running to him at night whenever he makes a peep and groveling to him the whole day." He came for parental guidance because his wife sent him. She, he obeys.

He enters the room hesitantly, twisting his shirt with his fingers, sits down in the armchair, his eyes darting all around. He's obviously feeling anxious. Is this his conscious third level of thinking? In their phone call a week earlier, the male therapist asked him to prepare for the meeting by writing down his dreams. In one dream he returns to his parents' home. The house is empty. The dishes in the sink are full of mold. This is an example of how our childhood returns to us in dreams and confirms what we knew without knowing it. Is this what Hugo felt as a child? An empty house? Often, as in this case, when a patient recounts his dreams, the therapist may feel that it gives him a better understanding of the patient than any description of real life. Why did Hugo have this particular dream a few days before the therapy session? Perhaps the upcoming session caused him to renew his unconscious thinking about himself and his past.

Having heard one dream, the therapist asks Hugo if he remembers other dreams. Hugo recalls that as a child he once dreamed that someone had shot him in the head. He woke up in fright and ran to his mother. Certainly an unpleasant dream, but not every child runs to his parents when they have a nightmare. Recently he dreamed that he was trying to play soccer, which he loves, but kept missing the ball. Other players were scoring elegant, magnificent goals to the delight of the cheering crowd, and also leaving a wonderful smell in their wake. After this he found himself alone at a party. He tells his therapist that he has been feeling lonely recently. In another dream, his wife has pictures in her wallet of famous people with whom she once had relationships. And in another dream, his wife is doing Botox and he joins her. Does he want to be like her?

Hugo's unconscious first level of thinking is revealed: anxiety, dependence, loneliness and a sense of inferiority. The therapist still feels unsure how to proceed with Hugo, and how to help him be a less threatened and more committed father. Hugo is indeed anxious and dependent in his unconscious first level of thinking, but why does he feel that he is his child's servant? This is rather an unusual thing to say. Perhaps it is even a little aggressive.

The therapist asks Hugo about his orgasm fantasy. Usually he leaves this for the end of the getting-acquainted session when more trust has developed. Hugo replies with a little smile, part awkward, part triumphant, that in this sphere he is in control. "I am standing up and she kneels and does fellatio on me or else she is on her stomach and I am on top of her. Just when I feel like a king and that she is serving me is when I come." Now it's clear why Hugo the king feels like a servant to his son. Hugo smiles. Deep down he seems to have known this all along. Hugo's recognition of the connection to his orgasm fantasy, to his default response, will help him avoid reacting out of it in his relationship with his son. Perhaps this orgasm fantasy was shaped in his relationship with his parent caregiver as a result of a feeling of inferiority in his unconscious first level of thinking; perhaps it arose mainly out of the actual encounter with the caregiving figure who let him feel like a king. None of that matters right now. What does matter is that Hugo identifies this part of his personality and understands the automatic behavior that it brings out in him.

The therapist asks if this default response characterizes Hugo in other situations, and recalls Hugo saying that his wife was the one who sent him for parental guidance. Evidently this is the dynamic between him and his wife. First he asks her questions that don't need to be asked, that he could answer himself, and then he retaliates in various ways for being dependent on her. For example, he suddenly forgets that it's his turn to look after the child, or he forgets other important things. Just happens to forget; anyone can forget things sometimes. But then he is in control, not a servant who receives orders from his wife but a king who decides when to stop forgetting. It seems that in his conscious third level of thinking, Hugo is also very dependent, just as in his unconscious first level of thinking. On this third level we know how anxious Hugo is, and the therapist also notes in their relationship how Hugo immediately trusts him. Anxiety, dependency and trust are all part of Hugo's conscious third level of thinking.

The therapist wishes to identify strengths in Hugo's conscious third level of thinking that will help him to become a better parent. He asks Hugo if he has recurrent daydreams, hoping that these will help Hugo to connect to and apply in the encounter with his son. It transpires that Hugo is quite a dreamy fellow. "Sometimes, I'm the greatest sprinter in history. I stand on the podium and receive the gold medal as the crowd cheers. In another daydream, I'm a stand-up comic performing before an audience that is laughing hysterically." The latter daydream will be more helpful, the therapist thinks, because it is more relationship-oriented, even though it is primarily narcissistic. Hugo clearly has strengths and ambitions in his daydreams but the therapist is looking for one that involves connection and compassion that Hugo may use to better relate to his son. Hugo also sometimes likes to imagine that he is a cool teacher that all the students love. This one sounds even better. Suddenly Hugo says that he sometimes pictures himself going back to his schooldays, and this time he is the one who accepts all the other kids who don't fit in and doesn't shun anyone. "This is the daydream you need to keep in mind when you are with your son," the therapist tells him. "You've got it!"

Later, the therapist will discuss with Hugo how he was the kid who didn't fit in and how he repressed this experience into his dream world, in compensation for which he creates a pleasant daydream in which he rescues children like himself. Now, however, his son is the rejected kid who doesn't fit in and he, Hugo, is rescuing him – just as in the daydream.

Hugo needs to relate to his son not through his orgasm fantasy of domination, but rather by means of a daydream in which he is strong and generous. In the absence of a warm-hearted daydream like this or a similar tendency in Hugo's conscious third level of thinking, the therapist would have had to work a lot harder to encourage such an attitude. In general, there are no good or bad fantasies. People need to connect to different parts of their personalities in order to succeed at various tasks. There could well be situations in which Hugo's orgasm fantasy is the correct response. For example, sometimes he needs to connect with his orgasm fantasy in order to stand up to his wife as someone deserving of respect, like a king, and not simply to accept whatever she says, as often happens. Hugo also wants to be the best in soccer, so connecting with his orgasm fantasy could help him be a king in that realm as well.

Improving sex and relationships

Hugo's wife likes to ride him and hold his hands tightly. When he is inside her she feels she is using him, exploiting him, and that he is helpless. Any moment now he will come without wanting to, which will drive her wild. This experience of seeing him simultaneously feeling pleasure and suffering while she orchestrates the entire symphony totally rocks her with pleasure. This is the trap that she sets; after all, he can't accuse her of rape. Hugo has told her he read that women can reach orgasm during rape but this doesn't alter the rapist's criminal liability. It's just a physiological response over which they have no control. Now when his wife "sexually exploits him," he imagines that he is the king and how different women must ride him in this way and he decides in whose vagina he wants to come. He imagines each woman impatiently watching the others, eager that they finish their ride and leave something for her. Sometimes he allots a limited time to each one, maybe just three or four "beats," as he calls them, no more. Justice is justice, and he is known as a king with a highly developed sense of fairness. Another woman then lifts her magnificent dress and sits astride him, watching him enjoy himself, but before she has achieved anything she has to make way for the next woman. Sometimes he asks his wife to go down on him while he is reading a book. Each one is doing their job, he says, and she turns out to be open to these games. This is how the kings behaved in their palaces, he says. They were occupied with royal business while different women competed to see who would win the honor of going down on the king while he was attending to the affairs of the kingdom. He recalls how Bill Clinton took an important phone call while Monica Lewinsky was giving him a blow job under the desk. "Now I'm Clinton," he announces. His wife is up for anything on condition that he lets her sexually exploit him afterwards.

The problem is that Hugo's wife is also very critical in her conscious third level of thinking. Her two upper levels of thinking thus reinforce each other and create aggressive responses that are hard for Hugo to deal with. Now when she rides him and he lets her use him just as she desires, she swears, sometimes to herself and sometimes out loud and without shame, especially in those tremendous moments just before orgasm and also in the first moments after the earthquake, that she realizes how aggressive and critical she can be and how she really needs to rein in this tendency, especially with someone who makes her feel so good and understands her and her needs so well. Lately too, Hugo has been reminding himself that because he is the king every night, it's okay for him to be less upset by her aggressiveness, since at night his true self will once again be revealed. And as for his son, he doesn't quite understand how it happened, but rather than feeling like an exploited servant, he recently feels quite good and generous.

2. Who Slept With Me?

Lucas and his wife Mila are desperate. Alexandra, their six-year-old daughter, is out of control in preschool. She hits and bites the other children, and they're all scared to death of her. "Nothing seems to affect her," says Lucas. "When the teacher praises her for something she acts up twice as much." Her parents can't understand it. They've never heard of anything like this, that a child who gets complimented acts more violently rather than being nicer. At home she may deliberately stick her hand under the knife when her father is slicing bread and straight away say it's his fault that she got hurt. When her mother has friends over Alexandra will announce in front of everyone that her mother has a big ass and that the other women in the room are much better mothers than she is. The parents are practically in tears. "Where did we go wrong?" they ask. In addition, Alexandra is a smart and pretty girl.

The female therapist listens. She understands that Alexandra is exhibiting sado-masochistic behavior. What child would deliberately insert her hand under a knife in order to accuse her father? What child would insult her mother this way in front of guests to evoke punishment from her? Sadomasochism could also explain why on receiving praise, Alexandra does everything to negate the compliment and the encouragement and convert it into punishment. This seems to be what she enjoys. Or more precisely, this is the type of relationship that she is familiar with. Good and warm relations? She's not interested. It could be a sign of weakness. Sadomasochistic relations are a real trap, because Alexandra really does anger everyone. They can't resist punishing her and then she calms down for a while because she got her wish – until the whole story repeats itself. How did this vicious cycle begin and how can it be stopped?

Lucas talks about his first level of thinking. In one of his dreams, Alexandra asks for permission to put makeup on him. At first he lets her but when he looks in the mirror and sees a woman he becomes furious. "She turns you into a girl," says the therapist and Lucas nods in agreement. In other dreams, Alexandra is chasing Lucas who is running away. She catches him, they struggle and he can't overpower her. In reality, when Lucas asks her to turn off the TV and go to bed Alexandra mocks him or doesn't answer him or just makes weird noises. In Lucas's conscious third level of thinking, he is filled with fury, which often appears in dreams in the form of a character that is mocking him or chasing him. He once had a dream in which she spat on him while he stood there helpless.

In truth, however, Lucas is not so helpless. Unlike what happens in his dream world, in real life he yells at Alexandra and punishes her severely for every little thing. For days he hasn't allowed her out of the house to play with friends, nor to touch her computer, and has also revoked permission for her to watch television. She is shut up in her room, but doesn't really seem to mind. Why is Lucas so tough on his daughter, the therapist wonders. Sometimes she thinks that Lucas's way of settling scores with Alexandra for every little thing is his way of educating her by ensuring that he is always in control.

When Lucas tells the therapist about his orgasm fantasy, things become clearer. He may be submissive in his unconscious first level of thinking, in his dreams, but not in his orgasm fantasy. "I'm not a rapist," Lucas says in an embarrassed tone. "The women cooperate with me because they have no choice. I am a famous gynecologist and if they want me to treat them they have to also let me enjoy. It seems totally fair to me. At least in fantasy," he adds with a little laugh. "So I control them thanks to my knowledge. In the correct order, I treat them first, and then I take my pleasure." The therapist can only imagine how Lucas pictures this. At least, they now both understand that the way Lucas acts with his daughter is informed by his aggressive orgasm fantasy. In his dreams he is offended by his daughter and in real life he activates his default response and attacks her. Thus far, it makes sense.

Later in therapy Lucas talks about his conscious third level of thinking, his recurrent daydreams. Here he is the prime minister, leading the country from one success to another, taking care of everyone in the difficult coronavirus days and beloved by everyone. Lucas's friends say that he's a really good guy, warm and always willing to help. Daydreams reflect part of our behavior. Is this daydream Lucas's "cure" for his aggressive orgasm fantasy? Possibly. His orgasm fantasy makes him feel guilty, for which he compensates in his daydream. This kind of relationship in the mind between the two conscious levels of thinking is quite common.

Lucas does, however, admit that he is scared of his wife. Mila says that he treats her with great respect even though she drives him crazy sometimes. In his dreams he is also fleeing from his wife who is chasing him. In one dream, she chases him, catches him and forces him to sleep with her. Another time, she forces him to sleep with the woman who lives next door. Lucas acknowledges that the truth is revealed in his dream world; he is afraid of both his daughter and his wife. But in real life, he behaves exactly the opposite towards them. He is very harsh towards his daughter, resulting from his orgasm fantasy, whereas with his wife he is all sweetness and light, like the benevolent prime minister.

Lucas's therapist works with him to change the mode of interaction with his daughter, not out of his aggressive orgasm fantasy but rather from his benevolent daydream. "You have it but you're not using it," she explains to him. "You just have to interact with your daughter in the same spirit of the prime minister who worries about the weak and needy people, from that good place inside you and not from your aggressive orgasm fantasy." The therapy work with Lucas was not difficult. Later Lucas admits that he just doesn't grasp how he could have been so aggressive toward his suffering daughter. "After all, she's part of me," he says with tears in his eyes.

Afterwards, they talked about how gentle and polite Lucas is with Mila. The therapist tries to gently encourage him to be more assertive with his wife, and to stand up for himself as he does in his aggressive orgasm fantasy. Mila admits that she nags him about lots of little things during the day and he feels that he dances to her tune. Maybe this is why he dreams that she is raping him, but even so, he still smiles at her like a good prime minister.

The riddle of Alexandra's sadomasochistic tendency, however, is still unsolved. For this, we need to turn to her mother, the person who was closest to her in her infancy. Mila says nonchalantly that her orgasm fantasy is to be deeply humiliated while she feels that the man is experiencing the most incredible pleasure. "Then, when he is at the peak of his pleasure and I am at the peak of my humiliation, that's when I reach orgasm." She has a fantasy in which different men with masks sleep with her and afterwards they remove the masks and she has to identify which one it was. In another fantasy she is examining the penises of the men standing naked in front of her, and has to figure out who slept with her. Mila says that the helplessness she feels when she has no idea which one of the men is coming inside her, while all the others stand around laughing, is what immediately makes her come.

During the day, Mila seems to reenact her orgasm fantasy with her daughter in many different ways without being aware of it. For example, she won't ask Alexandra nicely to give back the remote she took from her, but will snatch it away from her and shout that she had it first. In this way she leaves the child feeling hurt and invites her to take revenge. Another time, Alexandra might ask her politely for something and she won't respond, but if she asks her aggressively, she will immediately comply with her request. When Alexandra cries, Mila mocks her but when Alexandra orders her around, Mila surrenders. We have here behavior that matches the orgasm fantasy of a mother who is creating a similar fantasy of sadomasochistic relations in her daughter. We can't say exactly what Alexandra's orgasm fantasy will be a decade from now. The orgasm fantasy will be there in the latency stage; it will hint its presence in her unconscious behavior as it is doing now, until it breaks into her consciousness during adolescence. But now we understand how the orgasm fantasy develops in the delicate fabric that is woven between parent and child.

In the course of therapy, Alexandra and her parents drew much closer. Lucas began relating to Alexandra with the warmth and affection of his daydreams rather than playing into his daughter's sadomasochistic behavior patterns. The mother began to be aware of how she reenacts her orgasm fantasy in her relationship with her daughter. Previously, she didn't make the connection between the two issues. Now that she is fully aware of her orgasm fantasy, she tries to respond to her daughter not from a place of frustration but from a place of love and affection. Alexandra has gradually learned that human warmth really exists and that when she is weak it doesn't mean that people will laugh at her; rather, it means they will understand her. Now when she is praised, she may break into a smile. Or, at least, doesn't start hitting out in response. The therapist knows that Alexandra's orgasm fantasy has not changed but perhaps in her conscious third level of thinking, a new possibility of receiving warmth and love has been created. In regressive moments of anxiety and stress, she may still react out of her sadomasochistic orgasm fantasy, but just as her father learned to react from another place inside him and just as her mother learned to control her orgasm fantasy, Alexandra has also gradually learned to react not from the sadomasochistic place inside her but from a place that invites human connection.

Improving sex and relationships

Mila always told Lucas that she wants him to be more of a man, that he is kind of wimpy and she doesn't like it when he acts this way. It became clear that she was essentially inviting a sadomasochistic relationship with him too. She doesn't want him to be nice and gentle with her. "So what should I do?" Lucas asked her before they got into bed. "When I'm gentle with you and respond out of my conscious third level of thinking, out of my good daydreams, you attack me, and when I attack you against my will, you relax." The first gain for Mila and Lucas was in bed. Lucas loosened up and began to live his aggressive orgasm fantasy, which he had been afraid to do before. And Mila began to enjoy herself more and more. They laughed about it and this brought them much closer. "We're both nuts," Mila would say to him. "You're the pervert gynecologist and I'm the one who has to guess who had sex with me. Tell me, does that sound normal to you?" But, as often happens, closeness and pleasure in bed brought with it another gift that was just as valuable. Mila began to be aware of the kind of responses she was inviting from Lucas and he began to be aware that sometimes she does need him to be more forceful or, as she puts it, more of a man. But she can also accept him more as a soft and gentle man without it provoking her aggression. This delicate tango they dance together, each choosing from which place to respond to the other, continued to evolve, and kept them smiling together about how crazy they are.

1. WHY IS CONVERSION THERAPY SOMETIMES "SUCCESSFUL"?

The answer is simply because the patients were not homosexual to begin with. Rather, they fled from their heterosexual orgasm fantasy into homosexual relationships because the fantasy was unbearable for them. Some people use another defense mechanism of feeling that they do not have an orgasm fantasy and it often takes years for them to reveal and acknowledge it, the reason being that the content of the fantasy threatens their self-image, so the fantasy is repressed.

In her orgasm fantasy, Michelle sees a man threatening her with a knife. Just at the moment when the fear becomes too much to bear, she comes. With such a masochistic fantasy, this girl would surely invite others to hurt her. She developed an original method of doing so: she kept apologizing all the time, as if she'd done something really bad. In her apologies she adopted the position of victim and invited the other person to join her in a "tango" in which she really did behave badly. This behavior, it transpired, was basically a re-creation of the problematic relationship she had as a child with her abusive mother. Michelle's mother frequently blamed her and hit her and Michelle identified with these accusations. It's not surprising that in her conscious third level of thinking she feels tremendous fury that is often inappropriately directed at the people around her.

For years Michelle was involved in lesbian relationships. She was simply terrified by her orgasm fantasy, and presumably had an unconscious fear that she might re-create this orgasm fantasy in her relationship with a male partner and thereby invite abuse. Finally she met a gentle and sensitive guy who didn't fit her sexual fantasy and she married him. She compromised regarding her attraction to him, but felt that this way she could at least live without feeling threatened. On the other hand, she does seem to dominate him from her conscious third level of thinking.

Michelle started therapy at a time that she was involved in lesbian relationships. In the course of the therapy, she met her future husband. The therapist thinks he helped her change from a lesbian to a heterosexual. But the truth is that she was never really a lesbian.

❖ ❖ ❖

George proudly told his male therapist how open-minded and unprejudiced he is, and how he has no problem with homosexual relations. He had a boyfriend, and both mainly engaged in fellatio. In the course of therapy, George began to get close to women. He informed his therapist that he wished to have decent and respectful sexual relations with women and had an aversion to aggressive and degrading sex. Having repeated this statement several times, the therapist began to suspect that the term "respectful" actually obscured a considerable degree of aggression towards women. And indeed, later in therapy, his highly aggressive orgasm fantasy was revealed, one in which he brutally rapes women. At this point it became clear that this was his real orgasm fantasy that he finds the most arousing, and from which he fled into homosexual relationships. The fantasy naturally clashed with his self-image as a good person and he may also have feared that he might try to act on it. He therefore needed to escape from the fantasy, first into a homosexual relationship and later into "decent" relationships. From the therapist's perspective, however, the patient who came to him as a homosexual was "rehabilitated."

2. TRANSGENDERISM

The three levels of thinking influence sexual attraction and not just the orgasm fantasy. How do we appear in a dream, and how does the object of our attraction appear? On the conscious third level of thinking we may entertain romantic thoughts of different kinds. In this context, the orgasm fantasy can contain endless possibilities of attraction. The sky's the limit regarding the nature of the relationship that we create with our parents in earliest childhood, a relationship that will later evolve into an orgasm fantasy. This experience is far too rich and multilayered to be reduced to a simplistic and dichotomous division into heterosexual and homosexual attraction. The same applies to the way we ourselves appear in our orgasm fantasy. Women may appear as men and men as women. Sometimes we can observe sexual relations through the eyes of the opposite sex while residing in our own body. Some people may experience themselves with a penis and breasts, while others may be attracted to such figures. Many men can become highly aroused when wearing women's clothing and makeup while still being men in their experience. Certain women can become very aroused when they appear as men in their orgasm fantasy and have aggressive sexual relations with women or other men, with or without sex accessories to compensate for what is physically lacking. At the same time, these women may say that they like other female aspects of their personality in their conscious third level of thinking that they would never want to forgo. In their nighttime dreams or daydreams they may be attracted to different characters from those that appear in their orgasm fantasy. We understand that variation is endless not only regarding whom we're attracted to, but also regarding how we experience ourselves in the three levels of thinking. Throughout this book, we have seen several examples of this.

Consider the following example: A man who wants to undergo a sex-change operation has an orgasm fantasy in which a woman is dressing him in women's clothing and forcing him to be a woman. He wants to realize his orgasm fantasy but this is a masochistic fantasy! Perhaps he could be encouraged to realize it in the bedroom with his (male or female) partner. But why should he let the orgasm fantasy take over his whole life. We might say the same to a person with masochistic tendencies. Let him have as much pleasure as he can in bed, but in his daily life we will try to help him avoid inducing others to attack him and thereby realizing his orgasm fantasy that could hurt him.

Another example is a person who wishes to have a sex change operation and may later discover that the sex change was an attempted solution to his orgasm fantasy that was unbearable for him (as we saw in the previous chapter about conversion therapy). Does the same hold true for a man who in his orgasm fantasy sees himself as a woman making love to a man as it does for a man who in his orgasm fantasy is being forced to be a woman?

The orgasm fantasy, like nighttime dreams and daydreams, tells a story whose deep emotional significance can illuminate the inner truth a person is searching for. As a rule, the more aware of his emotions a person is and the more he is able to contain them, the less he will tend to be pushed towards behaviors arising from an absence of emotional awareness ("acting out" in professional jargon). Awareness of the three levels of thinking is thus crucially important and can be of particular help in cases of confusion or embarrassment regarding an individual's sexual identity or the object of his or her attraction.

3. RAPE

Why do some women who have been raped carry the trauma with them for many years, while others are less affected? Several variables may be involved. For example, a rape victim who is married and older will probably be less affected than a young woman or girl. Logically, the more experience a woman has had with sex, the lower the likelihood of severe trauma. But another key variable is apparently also at work here – the orgasm fantasy. A woman who is more connected to her sexuality and cognizant of her orgasm fantasy will probably be less affected than a woman who is repressing this fantasy. The repression could have more severe consequences when the orgasm fantasy involves rape, humiliation, masochism etc. The rape experience is especially difficult when the woman feels that something threatening from her unconscious is actually happening right before her eyes. The guilt feelings that we so often encounter in the wake of rape, and which may remain with the rape victim for many years, are related to her feeling that in some hidden private way she wanted it to happen. Women who have other non-masochistic orgasm fantasies would probably be less affected by rape because there would be no overlap between the rape and their orgasm fantasy. The psychological harm to the rape victim who has a masochistic orgasm fantasy (which many women do) of which she is unaware could take the form of a narrowing of her personality. Henceforth, she will be afraid to use her imagination, which constitutes very serious damage.

The conclusion to be drawn is that in cases of rape, sexual abuse, incest, etc., it is important to try to help the victim figure out, difficult as it may be, and with all due sensitivity, what her orgasm fantasy is. Of course, it must first be clearly explained to her that rape is a very serious crime that has no connection at all to the victim's orgasm fantasy. Even if her orgasm fantasy involves rape, degradation or something similar, it doesn't mean that this is what she wanted and would have chosen. Everyone has all kinds of nighttime dreams and daydreams and it doesn't mean that he or she wants them to come true. There are no forbidden thoughts, only forbidden acts. But for someone who has been sexually attacked, knowledge of her orgasm fantasy can release this repressed material and, along with it, also free the woman from guilt feelings and from the impulse toward a narrowing of thought. She need no longer be afraid to play with her thoughts, to be creative and imaginative. The closer people are to their orgasm fantasy, the more resilience they will have in the face of sexual abuse and rape.

One patient had an orgasm fantasy in which she was being raped in front of a crowd in a public place. She had never been raped, but both her parents were rather aggressive and imposing. She was afraid to sleep with her boyfriend and became filled with anxiety at the very idea. The boyfriend was warm and affectionate and for a year he did not pressure her to have sex. Gradually, the young woman was able to overcome her trauma and have sex with him. Each time before they had sex he would soothe and reassure her. Only when she was calm could she engage in her orgasm fantasy of rape and reach satisfaction. The ritual in which he soothes her because of her orgasm fantasy so that she can imagine it out of a sense of playfulness and security illustrates once again the emotional complexity surrounding this important fantasy. Indeed, in order to play with fantasies, one needs to feel secure in knowing that it is just a game.

4. Violence

We live in a violent world. If people with violent tendencies become aware of their orgasm fantasy, it will help them understand that it comes from them and not from their environment. In other words, it is not the situation that requires violence but rather the individual's personal disposition. By being aware of their orgasm fantasy, such people will come to recognize that they have a fixed personality trait, a tendency towards violence, which they need to be cognizant of.

In bed they may find boundless pleasure in this violent inclination, on condition that there is mutual consent and, of course, no physical harm is involved. The ability of these people to express their aggression via pleasurable sexual relations could actually enhance their awareness of this tendency and contribute to the release of the aggression. Above all, the orgasm fantasy invites a person to take responsibility because the individual suddenly understands the depth and intensity of his tendency (a violent tendency in this case) and also finds a good place to release it. I would recommend that all discussions of violence and attempts to reduce it (such as workshops for violent men, groups of prisoners, etc.) encourage the sharing of this fantasy without shame, as it can be a powerful tool in promoting the assumption of personal responsibility.

5. What If You're Attracted to the "Wrong" Type of Person?

A common complaint of both men and women is that they are not sexually attracted to someone they appreciate and think is the kind of person they would want to live with. For example, women who want a stable relationship with "nerdy" men but maintain that they aren't attracted to them. Men may be attracted to women who are overtly sexual and provocative, and less attracted to more reserved and "respectable" women with whom they would prefer to form a long-term relationship. A common complaint is "What can I do? I'm not attracted to her" or "I'm not attracted to him." In such situations, the couple can use their orgasm fantasies to help them see that attraction is something they have some control over rather than an inalterable fact.

In long-term relationships, many couples experience a decline in sexual desire, and at an older age various sexual

226

challenges may arise, such as difficulty getting or maintaining an erection, vaginal dryness and other problems. And, of course, depression, which is so commonplace in our world and that significantly suppresses sexual desire. These conditions can often be treated with medication.

The orgasm fantasy can help many couples to reawaken their sex lives and feel attracted to one another. Sometimes, the orgasm fantasy can even replace medication that increases sexual desire. Free and uninhibitedly open play with these fantasies can bring great pleasure to anyone. Bear in mind that the attraction we feel toward another person depends more on us than on them. The other person is a given but our imagination can be shaped and played with.

So instead of being fixated on different aspects of our partner that we don't like, we can focus on our orgasm fantasy. That way, it's all – or almost all – up to us!

6. Diagnostics and Pathologies

The various psychological and psychiatric diagnostic tools in use today (such as DSM and ICD) do not divide the personality into levels of thinking as the orgasm fantasy does. For this reason, the diagnosis remains overly general. For example, a person can be very independent on one level and very dependent on another. Similarly, some people may have masochistic tendencies at one level and sadistic tendencies at another, and it is important to understand from which level these two tendencies come. Moreover, the orgasm fantasy provides a diagnosis in the form of a story that is a more precise diagnosis than a single word. The same is true of a daydream or nighttime dream.

On the other hand, it would be interesting to consider how the various familiar diagnoses are reflected in the person's three levels of thinking. For example, people with a suicidal tendency would probably show a masochistic tendency in more than one level of thinking, which might intensify the tendency and reduce the ability to cope by means of competing fantasies. Narcissists would be easy to identify in different types of orgasm fantasies that place the individual at the center, etc.

BIBLIOGRAPHY

1. Adams-Silvan, A. (1986). The Active and Passive Fantasy of Rape as a Specific Determinant in a Case of Acrophobia. *Int. J. Psycho-Anal.*, 67:467-473
2. Adams-Silvan, A. and Silvan, M. (1994). Paradise Lost: A Case of Hysteria Illustrating a Specific Dynamic of Seduction Trauma. *Int. J. Psycho-Anal.*, 75:499-510.
3. Agass, D. (2000). Aspects of Narcissism in a Once-Weekly Psychotherapy. *Brit. J. Psychother*, 17(1):37-50.
4. Arbiser, S. (1994). The Man with the Bus Symptom. *Int. J. Psycho-Anal.*, 75:729-742
5. Baker, R. (1984). Some Considerations Arising from the Treatment of a Patient with Necrophilic Fantasies in Late Adolescence and Young Adulthood. *Int. J. Psycho-Anal.*, 65:283-294.
6. Balter, L. (2013). Discussion of Hermann Argelander's paper: 'The scenic function of the ego and its role in

symptom and character formation'. *Int. J. Psycho-Anal.*, 94(2):355-371

7. Bergmann, M.V. (1995). Observations on the Female Negative Oedipal Phase and its Significance in the Analytic Transference. *J. Clin. Psychoanal.*, 4(3):283-295.

8. Chessick, R.D. (1996). Impasse and Failure in Psychoanalytic Treatment. *J. Am. Acad. Psychoanal. Dyn. Psychiatr.*, 24(2):193-216

9. Coltart, N.E. (1985). The Treatment of a Transvestite. *Psychoanal. Psychother.*, 1(1):65-79

10. Dowling, S. (1990). Fantasy Formation: A Child Analyst's Perspective. *J. Amer. Psychoanal. Assn.*, 38:93-111

11. Eidelberg, L. (1945). A Contribution to the Study of the Masturbation Phantasy. *Int. J. Psycho-Anal.*, 26:127-137

12. Freud, A. (1923). The Relation of Beating-Phantasies to a Day-Dream. *Int. J. Psycho-Anal.*, 4:89-102

13. Freud, S. 1919 A child is being beaten. Standard Edition 17: 175-204 London: Hogarth Press, 1955

14. Friedman, S. (1999). A Type of Couple Sexual Dysfunction. *Psychoanal. Psychol.*, 16(1):76-87

15. Gabbard, G.O. (2007). 'Bound in a nutshell': Thoughts on complexity, reductionism, and 'infinite space.' *Int. J. Psycho-Anal.*, 88(3):559-574

16. Geleerd, E.R. (1957). Some Aspects of Psychoanalytic Technique in Adolescence. *Psychoanal. St. Child*, 12:263-283

17. Geleerd, E.R. (1958). Borderline States in Childhood and Adolescence. *Psychoanal. St. Child*, 13:279-295

18. Glenn, J. (1984). Psychic Trauma and Masochism. *J. Amer. Psychoanal. Assn.*, 32:357-386

19. Hägglund, T. (1980). Some Viewpoints on the Ego Ideal. *Int. Rev. Psycho-Anal.*, 7:207-218

20. Haesler, L. (1991). Relationship Between Extratransference Interpretations and Transference Interpretations: A Clinical Study. *Int. J. Psycho-Anal.*, 72:463-477

21. Hammerman, S. (1961). Masturbation and Character. *J. Amer. Psychoanal. Assn.*, 9:287-311

22. Hart, H.H. (1958). Maternal Narcissism and the Oedipus Complex. *Int. J. Psycho-Anal.*, 39:188-190

23. Heimann, P. (1975). From 'Cumulative Trauma' to *The Privacy of the Self—A Critical Review of M. Masud R. Khan's Book. Int. J. Psycho-Anal.*, 56:465-476

24. Hunt, W. (1973). Beating Fantasies and Daydreams Revisited: Presentation of a Case. *J. Amer. Psychoanal. Assn.*, 21:817-832

25. Hurst, D.M. (1996). Abstinence and Interaction. *Psychoanal. Inq.*, 16(1):78-87

26. Kavaler-Adler, S. (2003). Lesbian Homoerotic Transference in Dialectic with Developmental Mourning. *Psychoanal. Psychol.*, 20(1):131-152

27. Kohut, H. (1979). The Two Analyses of Mr Z. *Int. J. Psycho-Anal.*, 60:3-27

28. Kulish, N. and Holtzman, D. (2014). The Widening Scope of Indications for Perversion. *Psychoanal. Q.*, 83(2):281-313

29. Lax, R.F. (1977). The Role of Internalization in the Development of Certain Aspects of Female Masochism:

Ego Psychological Considerations. *Int. J. Psycho-Anal.*, 58:289-300

30. Laufer, M. (1968). The Body Image, the Function of Masturbation, and Adolescence—*Problems of the Ownership of the Body. Psychoanal. St. Child*, 23:114-137

31. Laufer, M. (1976). The Central Masturbation Fantasy, the Final Sexual Organization, and Adolescence. *Psychoanal. St. Child*, 31:297-316

32. Laufer, M.E. (1981). The Adolescent's Use of the Body in Object Relationships and in the Transference—*A Comparison of Borderline and Narcissistic Modes of Functioning. Psychoanal. St. Child*, 36:163-180

33. Laufer, M.E. (1982). Female Masturbation in Adolescence and the Development of the Relationship to the Body. *Int. J. Psycho-Anal.*, 63:295-302

34. McDougall, J. (1980). A Child is Being Eaten—*I: Psychosomatic States, Anxiety Neurosis and Hysteria—a Theoretical Approach* II: *The Abysmal Mother and the Cork Child—a Clinical Illustration. Contemp. Psychoanal.*, 16:417-459

35. Rudden, M. (2000). The Case of Ms. A. *J. Clin. Psychoanal.*, 9(3):371-389

36. Sloate, P.L. (2010). Superego and Sexuality: An Analysis of a Psychosomatic Solution. *Psychoanal. Inq.*, 30(5):457-473

37. Sprince, M.P. (1962). The Development of a Preoedipal Partnership Between an Adolescent Girl and her Mother. *Psychoanal. St. Child*, 17:418-450

38. Welsh, S.S. (1998). The Case of Ms. A. *J. Clin. Psychoanal.*, 7(1):127-163

39. Wilkinson, M. (2001). His mother-tongue. *J. Anal. Psychol.*, 46(2):257-273

40. Wright, J. (2000). Discussion. *J. Clin. Psychoanal.*, 9(3):390-399

41. Wurmser, L. (1995). Chapter 3: Compulsiveness and Conflict: The Distinction Between Description and Explanation in the Treatment of Addictive Behavior. *The Psychology and Treatment of Addictive Behavior*, 43-64